D1611200

UNSER

An American Family Portrait

by
Gordon Kirby

Author:
Gordon Kirby

Editor:
Leslie Ann Taylor

Design and Production:
Marvenco, Inc.
San Ramon, California

Printed by:
Hunter Publishing Company
Winston-Salem, North Carolina

Published by:
Anlon Press
Dallas, Texas

In The United States
Distributed to the Trade by:
Henry Holt and Company
115 West 18th Street
New York, New York 10011

In Canada
Distributed by:
Fitzhenry & Whiteside Limited
195 Allstate Parkway
Markham, Ontario
Canada L3R 4T8

ISBN 0-916105-03-2

Contents

COURSE OF THE Pikes Peak AUTO HILL CLIMB

SUMMIT OF PIKES PEAK FINISH

MILE 20
MILE 19
MILE 18
MILE 17
MILE 16
MILE 15
MILE 14
MILE 13
MILE 12
MILE 11
MILE 10
MILE 9
MILE 8
MILE 7

DEVILS PLAYGROUND PARKING
BEST VIEW OF RACE

Glen Cove LUNCHES PARKING

BROWN BUSH CORNER

HALF-WAY CAMP GROUND

START OF RACE

N

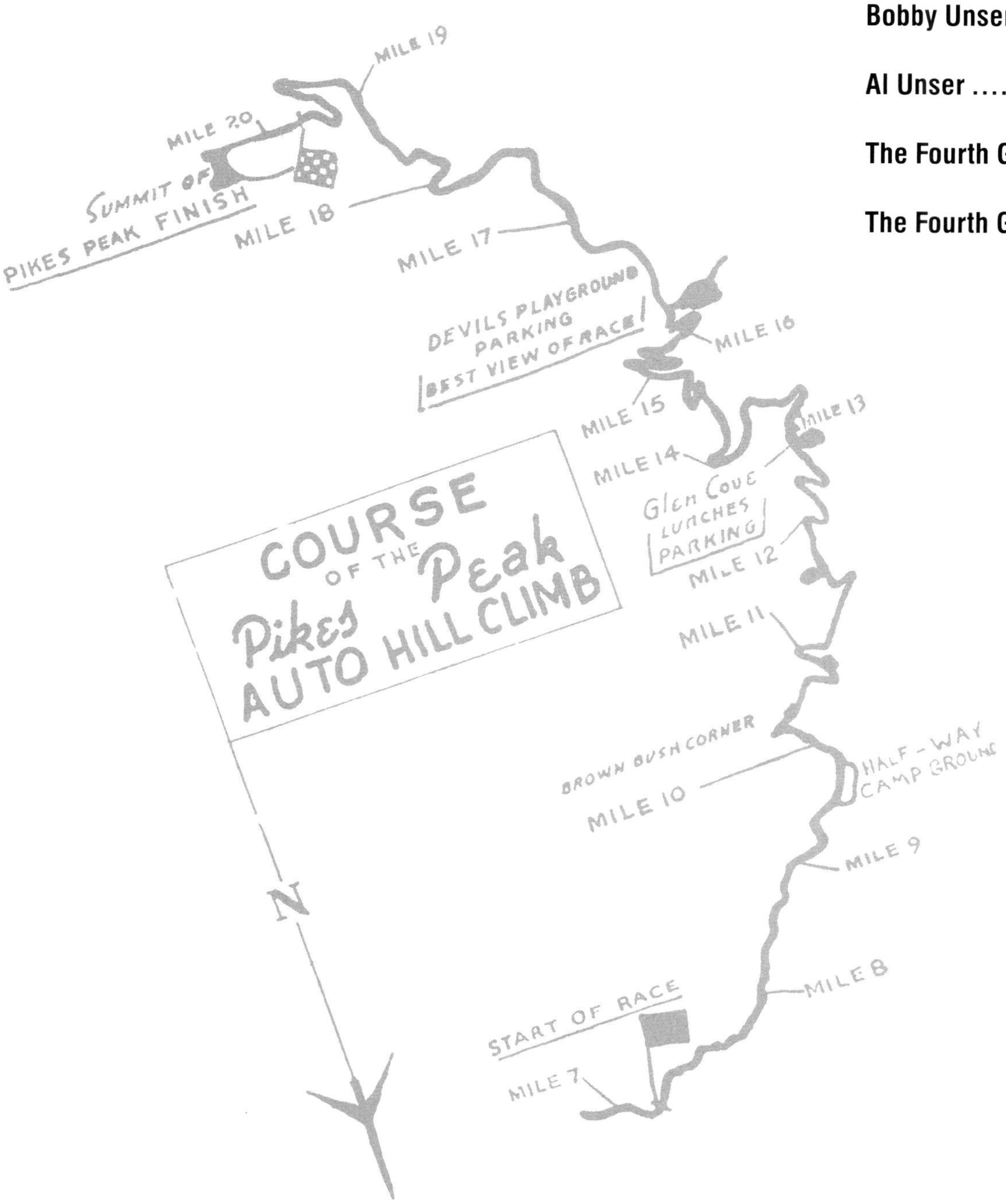

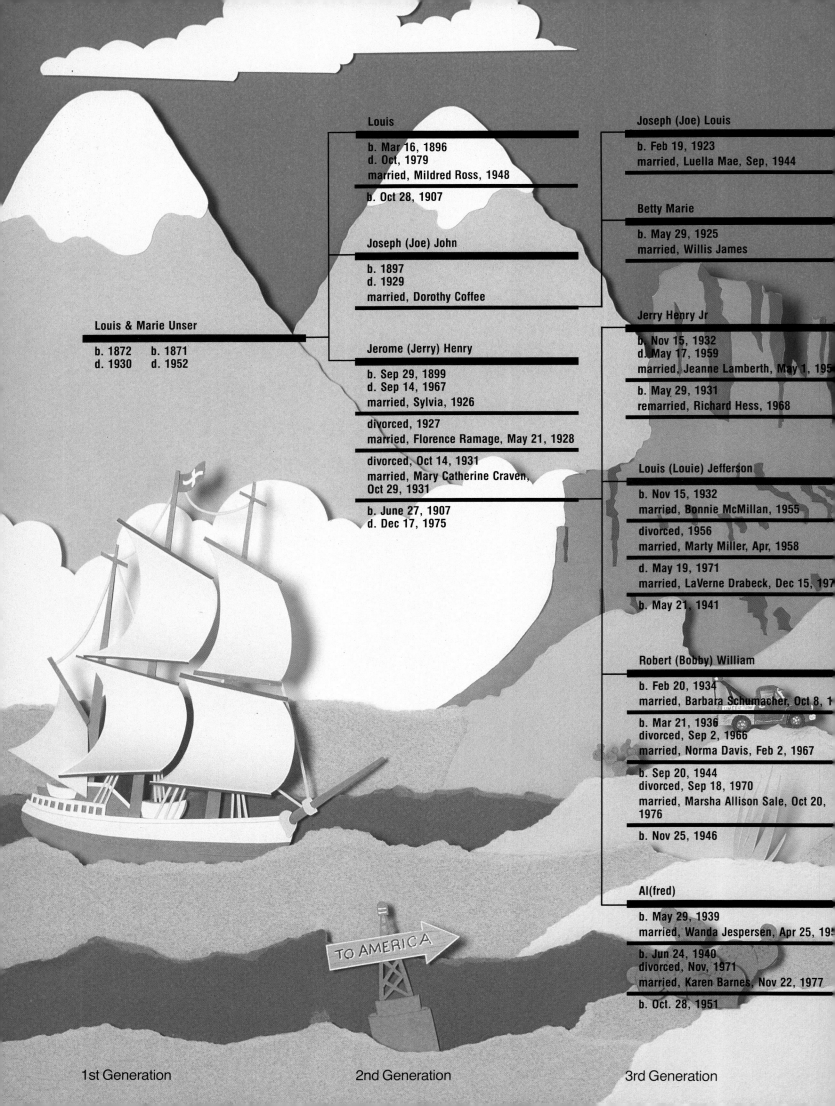

Louis & Marie Unser

b. 1872   b. 1871
d. 1930   d. 1952

Louis

b. Mar 16, 1896
d. Oct, 1979
married, Mildred Ross, 1948

b. Oct 28, 1907

Joseph (Joe) John

b. 1897
d. 1929
married, Dorothy Coffee

Jerome (Jerry) Henry

b. Sep 29, 1899
d. Sep 14, 1967
married, Sylvia, 1926

divorced, 1927
married, Florence Ramage, May 21, 1928

divorced, Oct 14, 1931
married, Mary Catherine Craven,
Oct 29, 1931

b. June 27, 1907
d. Dec 17, 1975

Joseph (Joe) Louis

b. Feb 19, 1923
married, Luella Mae, Sep, 1944

Betty Marie

b. May 29, 1925
married, Willis James

Jerry Henry Jr

b. Nov 15, 1932
d. May 17, 1959
married, Jeanne Lamberth, May 1, 195

b. May 29, 1931
remarried, Richard Hess, 1968

Louis (Louie) Jefferson

b. Nov 15, 1932
married, Bonnie McMillan, 1955

divorced, 1956
married, Marty Miller, Apr, 1958

d. May 19, 1971
married, LaVerne Drabeck, Dec 15, 197

b. May 21, 1941

Robert (Bobby) William

b. Feb 20, 1934
married, Barbara Schumacher, Oct 8, 1

b. Mar 21, 1936
divorced, Sep 2, 1966
married, Norma Davis, Feb 2, 1967

b. Sep 20, 1944
divorced, Sep 18, 1970
married, Marsha Allison Sale, Oct 20,
1976

b. Nov 25, 1946

Al(fred)

b. May 29, 1939
married, Wanda Jespersen, Apr 25, 195

b. Jun 24, 1940
divorced, Nov, 1971
married, Karen Barnes, Nov 22, 1977

b. Oct. 28, 1951

TO AMERICA

1st Generation   2nd Generation   3rd Generation

Unser Family Tree

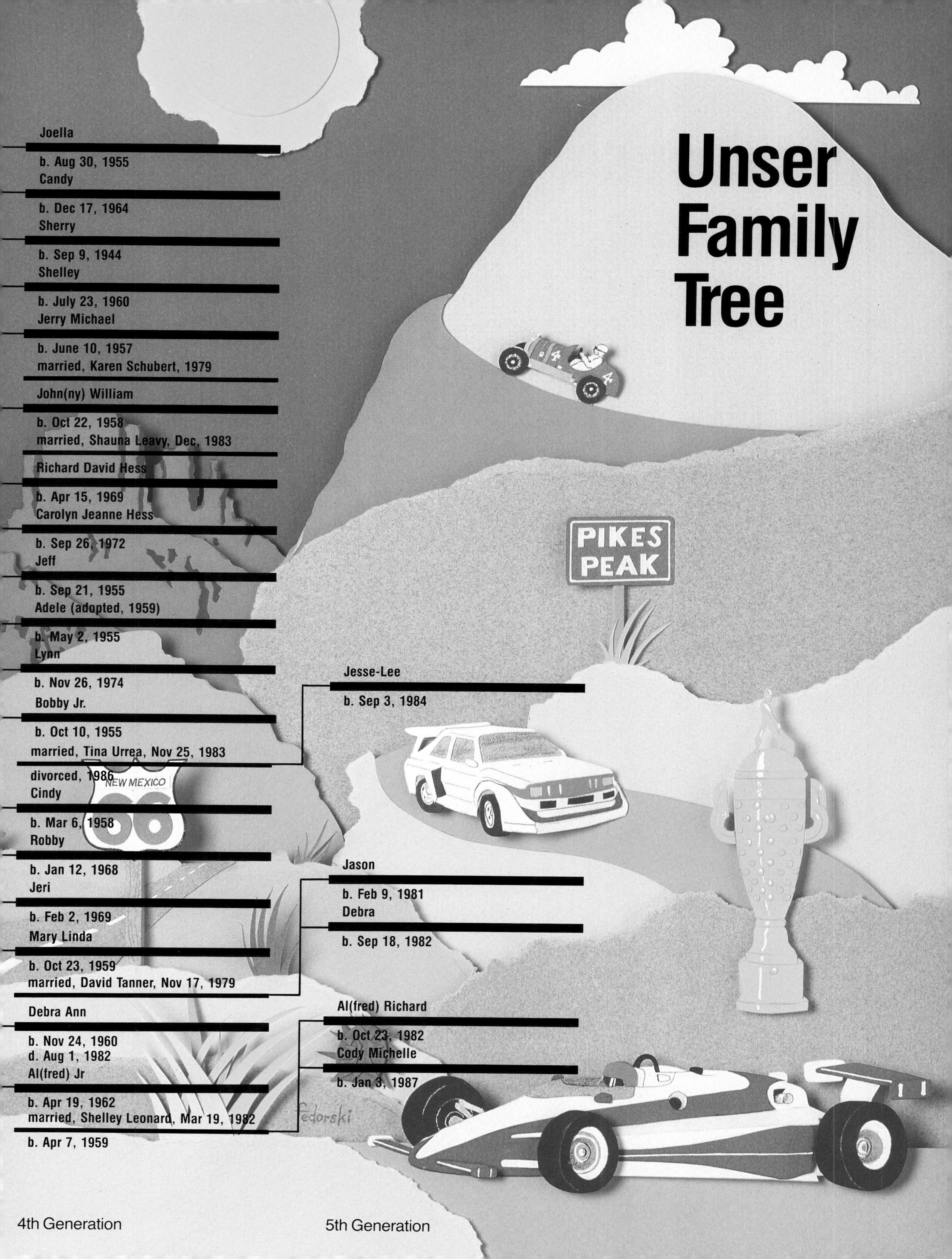

Joella
b. Aug 30, 1955

Candy
b. Dec 17, 1964

Sherry
b. Sep 9, 1944

Shelley
b. July 23, 1960

Jerry Michael
b. June 10, 1957
married, Karen Schubert, 1979

John(ny) William
b. Oct 22, 1958
married, Shauna Leavy, Dec, 1983

Richard David Hess
b. Apr 15, 1969

Carolyn Jeanne Hess
b. Sep 26, 1972

Jeff
b. Sep 21, 1955

Adele (adopted, 1959)
b. May 2, 1955

Lynn
b. Nov 26, 1974

Bobby Jr.
b. Oct 10, 1955
married, Tina Urrea, Nov 25, 1983
divorced, 1986

Cindy
b. Mar 6, 1958

Robby
b. Jan 12, 1968

Jeri
b. Feb 2, 1969

Mary Linda
b. Oct 23, 1959
married, David Tanner, Nov 17, 1979

Debra Ann
b. Nov 24, 1960
d. Aug 1, 1982

Al(fred) Jr
b. Apr 19, 1962
married, Shelley Leonard, Mar 19, 1982
b. Apr 7, 1959

Jesse-Lee
b. Sep 3, 1984

Jason
b. Feb 9, 1981

Debra
b. Sep 18, 1982

Al(fred) Richard
b. Oct 23, 1982

Cody Michelle
b. Jan 3, 1987

PIKES PEAK

NEW MEXICO 66

4th Generation

5th Generation

Introduction

Regret has long been a favorite topic for the poets and scribes. But not one has ever touched upon a regret I have. I regret that I didn't meet the Unsers sooner. At this point (since the introduction to a book is always written after the book is finished), I feel as if I've known the entire family, all five generations, since they first set foot in the United States. Oh, if that could only be true.

I first met three of the Unsers—Louie, Bobby and Al—when I was a motorsports journalist in Southern California in the mid-seventies. They, I'm afraid, had progressed much farther in their fields than I in mine. To my basic "What do you think" and "How does it feel" questions, they gave insightful, thought-provoking answers. They took time with a relative neophyte. And I think it's right about then that I started pondering a way to share the Unsers with the rest of the world.

In truth, I was impressed by more than what I interpreted to be their compassion for a newcomer. My opinion was also influenced by the regard in which they were, and are, held by their peers. Two such men share their thoughts about the Unsers.

AJ Foyt is of the opinion that, "The Unser family has been very good for racing. The whole family has really been an example of what racing is all about. The first I heard of them was at Pike's Peak. They owned the hill. They are good, tough competitors. There's never been a family like them.

"If I didn't think a whole lot of the Unsers I wouldn't ask them to co-drive with me in my Porsche long-distance car. Of course, I took the risk on Al the first time he qualified at the Speedway and I've had him drive for me a couple of times in my long-distance cars. Now I've got Al Junior driving for me. He's a heckuva driver and a fine young man."

"I was lucky enough to know their dad and their mother," Mario Andretti remembers. "It was always such a competitive family. I knew all the brothers except Jerry, and if you want to talk about an example of a true racing family, then the Unsers are it. The entire family has always been totally supportive of racing. I remember when Bobby and Al were in their twenties coming up through the ranks, and seeing how much support they had from their mom and dad. When you look back at the whole family, they've had tremendous success coupled with some tragedy.

"I've been very friendly with the whole bunch of them. Over the years we've had a lot of quality times together, both with Bobby and Al. I've been teammates with both of them at different times. We basically come from the same generation, and those are the guys I've really learned to appreciate over the years. They're the guys who produced most of the competition for me over the years and they're still there, cultivating their young ones the same way I have been. I guess I've been mirroring some of my situation with my kids and appreciating a lot of the trials and tribulations that the Unsers have gone through because a lot of it has also been happening to me. We have a lot in common, except we have no sagebrush here in Pennsylvania!

"I won the only time I ran at Pike's Peak and that was in Bobby's car. If it hadn't been for Bobby, I wouldn't have run there at all. He demanded that I do it. He didn't ask. He just said, 'You're gonna do it.' He gave me a first-class shot at it. It was fun. He showed me all he wanted to show me, and I won because he was not competing in the Championship class. He was running only in a stock car that year. That was part of the deal. We had some good times together, memorable times."

And that's the third thing about the Unsers that captivated me. The family delights in a good time. For each victorious peak captured by an Unser, there seems to have been at least an equal number of valleys. But the Unsers don't dwell on the rough times. They seem to take them in, deal with them and put them aside. As Bobby said recently, "It's the good Lord's will."

The fourth thing that makes this clan extraordinary is the women. To be the wife—or mother—of a professional race driver is a role that demands exceptional depth and understanding and a strong sense of humor. I never met Mom Unser. However, from all that I've read about Mom, she'd be as pleased as can be at the way Marsha has not only fulfilled the role of Bobby's wife, but also that of family matriarch. Al Junior's wife, Shelley, seems to be shaped of the same cloth, from a bolt all too seldom used.

What a family this is! Each member different than the others, yet a binding similarity to all. And I'm absolutely delighted that you're going to have a chance to meet them. But before you do, I would like to thank author Gordon Kirby for sharing the knowledge gleaned through many years of friendship with the Unsers. And both Gordon and I feel it imperative to let you know that, without the cooperation of all the Unsers, this book would have been impossible. To one and all, thank you for your time and energy. Would that there was a phrase even more grateful than, "Thank you." This would be the phrase Gordon and I would address to Marsha and Bobby. Their helpfulness, encouragement and hospitality were unflagging. Thank you both.

Now, before this begins to sound like the Academy Awards, I'm proud to introduce you to the Unsers, an American family.

Leslie Ann Taylor
March 12, 1988
New Milford, Connecticut

Author's Acknowledgements

I can only echo Leslie Ann's thanks to the Unser family and to Bobby and Marsha in particular for their invaluable advice and assistance. My thanks also to Leslie Ann for her enthusiastic, unflagging efforts and to photographer Bob Tronolone for access to his excellent historical file.

Finally, I would like to extend my thanks also to Jon Tedesco and his staff, Vera, Liza, Patty, Richard, Ramona, Cheryl, Adriana and Nancy for their hard work under the all-too-familiar pressure of deadlines.

Gordon Kirby,
Chocorua, New Hampshire, March 1988.

"This is my grandmother, Marie,
Daddy's mother."
BOBBY UNSER
Photo Courtesy of the Unser Family

JOE, JERRY and LOUIS UNSER
Photo Courtesy of the Unser Family

The Beginning

Photographed in 1934, Jerry Unser, Sr., father of Jerry, Louie, Bobby, and Al called on his own experiences when coaching his sons in driving Pike's Peak.
Photo Courtesy of the Unser Family

Jerry, Al, Louie, and Bobby looking their best in 1944.

Among the multitudes thronging Ellis Island in the late 1800s was a young couple from northern Switzerland, Louis and Marie Unser. Having passed the scrutiny and survived the interrogation to which almost all immigrants were subjected, the Unsers took their meager belongings and unlimited dreams westward to the Mississippi River town of Alton, Illinois. Perhaps this place was too settled or had too many boundaries to provide the freedom that unlimited dreaming demands. Louis and Marie once again packed up and continued their journey west. Automobiles were just beginning to appear on the landscape of American life when Louis and Marie Unser settled in Colorado Springs and started to raise a family. The Unser dynasty and accompanying legend had begun.

Louis Unser earned a living by his wits and his hands. He was a butcher by trade but, like many other settlers, he was a jack-of-all-trades—one who, it developed, was especially skilled in exploring and solving the mysteries of the new-fangled automobile engine. Together, Louis and Marie raised three sons: Louis, Jr., Jerome (Jerry), and Joseph (Joe). They grew up in Colorado Springs, learning from their father about machines and automobiles.

As the three Unser youngsters grew up, they were taken with the idea of motoring up a nearby mountain named Pike's Peak—so-named in honor of U.S. Army Lieutenant Zebulon Pike, a man foolish enough to declare, upon encountering the mountain in 1806, that the rocky peak would never be scaled. (Only fourteen years later he was proved wrong when adventurer Edwin Jones reached the 14,110-foot summit.) The Unser boys could not resist the lure of doing the improbable. So, in September of 1915, they rode a motorcycle and sidecar to the summit. Just like that, no big deal. Just one of the many Unser "firsts."

Of course, the Unser brothers were more than just a little familiar with the motorcycle. Such was their expertise that the Colorado City police hired all three to teach the police force how to ride the two-wheeled vehicles.

In any event, around the same time as the motorcycle conquest of "their" hill, local philanthropist Spencer Penrose decided to spend $500,000 to build a proper road up Pike's Peak, and, in 1916, Penrose officially christened the road by staging a "Race to the Clouds." The first 12.4-mile race to the top of Pike's Peak was won by Rea Lentz in just under 21 minutes. Louis', Jerry's and Joe's dreams of taking command of the mountain almost in their back yard were then put on hold by World War I. However, when the race resumed on an annual basis in 1920, the Unser boys quickly became regular competitors.

Of the three, younger brother Joe was the best driver. He showed it by finishing second at Pike's Peak in four consecutive runnings of the race, 1926-29. Bobby Unser, the patriarch of today's racing Unser family, pays Joe the finest compliment: "From everything I was always told," says Bobby, "Uncle Joe was probably the best race car driver of the three of them. The way the story was always told to me, Joe was a fast, smart, aggressive driver."

"This is Uncle Joe."
BOBBY UNSER
Photo Courtesy of the Unser Family

The matriarch of the American Unsers, Marie, takes a moment with son Louis.
Photo Courtesy of the Unser Family

12

In 1936, Jerry finished third at Pike's Peak.
Photo Courtesy of the Unser Family

THE COLORADO SPRINGS

C.S. SAILOR IS COMMENDED

Jerome Unser Praised for Heroism in Fire on Sub Chaser

Jerome Unser, son of Mrs. Mary Unser, 2724 West Colorado avenue, who has served in the United States navy for the last two years, has been officially commended by the navy department for heroism, according to a telegram received here at the local navy recruiting office from the navy headquarters at Washington.

The telegram, which tells the story, is as follows:

"Jerome Henry Unser, machinist's mate, first class, U. S. navy, of the U. S. ship Chilbowe, whose mother, Mary Unser, resides at 2724 Colorado avenue, Colorado Springs, has been commended by the navy department, with two other men, for his prompt and heroic action on April 25, 1919, on board the U. S. subchaser No. 20, when the starboard engine backfired, blowing off the tin deflector from the vaporizer and setting fire to the floor boards. Unser enlisted April 21, 1917."

"This was the submarine chaser Daddy was on—the one he was on when he earned a medal for bravery."
BOBBY UNSER
Photo Courtesy of the Unser Family

In 1929, Jerome and Marie's sons, (left to right) Jerry, Louis and Joe, had high hopes of conquering the Indianapolis 500—hopes that were smashed when Joe was killed testing the car in which he was photographed.
Photo Courtesy of the Unser Family

13

A $5,000 award was strong motivation for Jerry to attempt to answer the challenge of the American Gyro Company in 1932: Drive round trip between Denver and Los Angeles in 48 hours. The first leg of the trip was relatively uneventful. He dutifully stopped in every town and, so as to prove he was not taking shortcuts, wired his location. Engine problems in Los Angeles, however, delayed the start of his return trip—time he was determined to make up on the road. When he reached the Utah state line, the police were waiting. "Obey the speed limit or go to jail," was the edict.

"I drove across Utah at 60 miles an hour, mad as hops, with the state troopers right behind me," Jerry said. "At the Wyoming border, I hit a blinding snow storm. I could hardly see my radiator cap. Just the same I floor-boarded the accelerator and crossed Wyoming at 120 miles an hour. My biggest job was keeping my co-driver from jumping out of the car. He wound up the trip with a nervous breakdown, but we got to Denver at the end of 47 hours and 43 minutes."

Seeking some diversification, after the 1929 Pike's Peak race, the Unser boys decided they were going to tackle America's most famous auto race, the Indianapolis 500. They began preparing three powerful monsters for the assault on Indianapolis, but disaster struck when Joe crashed and was killed while testing one of the Coleman race cars on a Colorado highway. Brother Jerry later recalled, "All three of us were getting ready for Indianapolis, but after Joe's accident, the Coleman Front Drive Company withdrew its sponsorship. I never did get to race at Indianapolis." The family's plan to

head east to Indianapolis was put on the shelf until, many years later, Jerry's sons completed the journey.

King of the Peak in those early days was Glen Shultz, who won the rugged mountainside climb seven times between 1923 and '33—usually chased hard by an Unser. Brothers Louis and Jerry continued to race at Pike's Peak. In 1930, Louis finished second to Glen Shultz, and the following year Jerry came home in third place.

Then, in 1934, at the wheel of one of Shultz's cars, Louis finally won the "Race to the Clouds," in record time, too. The race wasn't run in 1935—the depths of the Depression—but Louis dominated from 1935-41, losing only once to arch-rival Al Rogers in 1940. There were no races from 1942-45 because of World War II. After the war, Louis picked up where he had left off, winning, in 1946 and '47, the first two post-war climbs up the Peak. Six years later, at 57, Louis won his ninth and last Pike's Peak climb, yet again setting a new record.

CUMMINS MAKES YOU A WINNER

At Indy, and On the Interstate

- In the 1987 Indy 500, Al Unser drove his Cummins-sponsored race car, with a Cummins turbocharger, into Victory Circle, and into the record books as a four-time winner of racing's Greatest Spectacle.
- Experience, quality engineering and total commitment make the winning difference at Indy and on the Interstate.

CUMMINS 444 **NTC-400**

- Over 1 million Cummins-powered trucks are running today. • Cummins has new Big Power NT engines at 365, 400 and 444 horsepower. Every day, every mile, you win with dependable, fuel efficient, high performance, high resale value engines. • Call your Cummins Distributor or Truck Dealer today. • Let Cummins make you a winner!

Louis earned his living as an automotive machinist. He married Mildred Ross and lived in Colorado Springs, finding success at Pike's Peak in cars other than his own. Many of Louis' victories at Pike's Peak were scored in Russ Snowberger's Federal Engineering cars, including the Maserati he drove in 1946 and '47.

"Uncle Louis was an exceptionally good machinist," says family patriarch Bobby. "He was a perfectionist, but he couldn't tune-up an engine or a race car. Uncle Louis didn't know how to set up a car. He got himself the right rides and drove them well while my daddy (Jerry) always built and worked on his own cars."

The brothers differed in other ways, also. Unlike Louis, brother Jerry was filled with wanderlust. Even though he raced regularly at Pike's Peak, he lived elsewhere for much of his early years. Just as the mysteries of the automobile had captured his father, the mystery of the airplane captured Jerry. He hooked up with a barnstormer named Clevenger and toured the country. He flew until he lost his pilot's license for over-exuberant stunts, then acted as a mechanic until he lost that license for souping up an engine before a race. Ever an Unser, he questioned the logic of racing if you had a limit on engine speeds.

Jerry served with distinction in the U.S. Navy during World War I, and after the war lived in various places in California and Arizona, returning occasionally to Colorado Springs. In 1927 he was Castro Valley, California's first fire chief and was married for a short period of time to a woman named Sylvia. After divorcing Sylvia, Jerry was remarried in 1928 to Florence Ramage. Two years later, still in

California, Jerry was again divorced. Jerry received bumps and bruises from more than his marital life while in California. Having devoted a great deal of his young life to building cars and making them go faster, he transferred his automotive knowledge into walking away from a wide variety of crashes. Jerry became a movie stunt driver.

In 1931, having survived his California experience, Jerry was living in Colorado Springs when he met Mary Craven, a well-bred young lady from Springfield, Missouri. Mary was an accomplished pianist who had studied music at a women's college near St. Louis. Suffering from hay fever, she spent the summer of 1931 with relatives in Colorado Springs and met Jerry Unser at a party. Back home, Mary

"This is a close up of us three boys—(left to right) me, Louie and Jerry. We just found these two pictures recently. They came from a lady who brought them to me at Pike's Peak this past year (1987)."
BOBBY UNSER
Photo Courtesy of the Unser Family

17

"This is in Colorado, before we moved to Albuquerque. This is (left to right) Daddy, me, Louie, Jerry, and Mom."
BOBBY UNSER
Photo Courtesy of the Unser Family

Craven was engaged to a respected local citizen but that didn't overly impress Jerry, always a man who knew what he wanted. It didn't take long for Jerry and Mary to elope.

Mary used to say her courtship with Jerry was "one of the strangest you could imagine." The couple passed most of their early dates together in Jerry's garage while Jerry worked on his race car. Jerry's method and style of living, as well as his eloping with Mary, meant that for many years the Craven family wasn't very happy with its new son-in-law.

Jerry and his new bride lived in Colorado Springs for a few years, although Jerry was often on the road in search of work. In November, 1932, Mary bore Jerry a pair of twin sons, Jerry Junior and Louis. Fifteen months later, Bobby was born. In 1936, Jerry moved his young family south to Albuquerque, aiming to settle down for good. Albuquerque, located in the middle of New Mexico on U.S. Route 66 as the highway heads west from the Texas panhandle into Arizona and ultimately to California, seemed to Jerry Unser the ideal place for a man to earn a living in the automobile repair business. After moving to Albuquerque, Jerry never again raced at Pike's Peak, although he was to return 20 years later with three of his four sons, beginning another chapter in the history of both the Peak and the Unser family.

In Albuquerque, Jerry first opened a small garage at the intersection of Rio Grande and Central Avenues on the outskirts of downtown. Later he moved a few miles farther out, operating both a

Uncle Louis poses during one of his pre-World War II runs at Pike's Peak.
Photo Courtesy of the Unser Family

garage and a filling station. Finally, in 1940, Jerry found the ideal place to set up business. He established his business and his home on the western end of Central Avenue (also known as Route 66), where the road climbs Albuquerque's west mesa after crossing the Rio Grande. Driving west on Route 66 out of Albuquerque, Jerry Unser's place was the last garage you passed.

"That was Daddy's strategy," explains Bobby, "to be on the edge of town where people would always know where you were. And of course, it would be a place to pull into if you were having trouble with your car.

"Daddy could do anything and everything," Bobby declares. "He could build houses, cars, engines. He could do fabrication work, plumbing, carpentry. He was really good with slide rules and trigonometry. And it was all self-taught because he never had more than an eighth-grade education.

"Uncle Louis used to come and visit once a year," Bobby tells the story. "And we used to look forward to that more than anything you could imagine. Uncle Louis always drove nice cars and dressed well. We always thought of Uncle Louis as being rich. Daddy was always poor, we knew that, and to us kids Uncle Louis seemed rich."

But "poor" or not, Jerry was determined to instill in his sons the knowledge his father had given him. Eight years old when he learned to drive, Jerry knew that the 11-year-old twins and 10-year-old Bobby were ripe to learn the automotive art. He traded the boy's donkeys for a Model A Ford. The accompanying rules forbade highway driving of any sort. So the boys trained along burro trails out on the mesa.

The Unser men pose in front of the shop in 1940: (left to right) Jerry, Louie, Daddy holding up Al, and Bobby.
Photo Courtesy of the Unser Family

"That's Daddy on the top, Mom, Louie, Jerry, Al, and me. This was our cabin in the mountains on the edge of Albuquerque—on the backside, the eastern side of the mountains. We all built this ourselves. Building that house *and* building the road going into it, was one of the hardest things I've *ever* done: a rough job.

"The summer there was a polio epidemic in Albuquerque and Daddy loaded us all in the car—this is where we spent the entire summer."

BOBBY UNSER
Photo Courtesy of the Unser Family

One of Marie Unser's treasures:
a photograph of her son, Louis.
Photo Courtesy of the Unser Family

Louis poses with his Pike's Peak mechanic Russ Snowberger.
Photo Courtesy of the Unser Family

At the wheel of the Russ Snowberger's Federal Engineering car, Louis has his hands full crossing the Pike's Peak finish line—backwards!
Photo Courtesy of the Unser Family

22

"This is (left to right) Jerry on Silver, Louie and Bud Stagner, who's on my donkey. Bud was Daddy's shop foreman and like a second father to us boys. Bud raised us during our real early years."

BOBBY UNSER

Photo Courtesy of the Unser Family

"This was our first deer hunt. We went down to Magdalena, New Mexico. This is (left to right) Jerry, Daddy, Louie, me, and Al. And that's the buck that Daddy shot."

BOBBY UNSER

Photo Courtesy of the Unser Family

Jerry and Mary's fourth son Alfred (Al) was born in 1939. Two years later the terror of a polio epidemic swept Albuquerque. Jerry, never foolish enough to panic but wise enough to recognize a threat to his family's well being, loaded up the boys and moved them into the mountains surrounding the city.

Removed from the horror of polio, the summer turned into a time of enchantment, one which Bobby remembers today with a warm smile. "We lived in the high mountains on a lake," says Bobby. "We were 35 miles from town and there was no electricity. We fished for our food every day. Daddy was also a very good hunter. He was amazing. He never pulled the trigger without something falling."

"This is Bud Stagner. He was a driver, not a successful racing driver, but he definitely was a driver."

BOBBY UNSER

Photo Courtesy of the Unser Family

It wasn't long before his "foreign car" repair shop, out on the beginnings of the west mesa, was thriving. "Daddy could fix things nobody else could," says Bobby. "Frank Lloyd Wright, for example, used to bring his cars to Daddy. He had all kinds of weird cars and nobody could work on them. As kids we had to work on all the different cars that came into Daddy's shop, so it was a great education for us. We classified all the many cars we worked on as foreign cars, because they were all out of the ordinary."

Having practiced on the Model A, Jerry's boys were soon behind the wheels of race cars, the older three running races before they turned 16. He summed up his philosophy of racing which he instilled in his sons, "I don't make them feel they have to be first, only that they do their best. Racing is a great sport and it should be participated in greatly."

Like their father, the boys were strong-willed and adventurous. It was not unheard of for any one of them to incur their father's wrath, and when they did, they knew about it immediately. "My kids learned long ago how to take a chewing-out gracefully," Jerry once explained. "When anyone asks me how come my kids make so few mistakes, I tell them, 'If you'd been chewed out as often as they had, you wouldn't make many mistakes either.' The kids don't mind. They know I'm not stingy with my praise, either."

Furthermore, Jerry never asked for more than he gave. He defined the absolute commitment he knew was necessary by showing them his own example of endless hours of work. Bobby: "Daddy worked every day until midnight for years. Then he started closing-down at ten o'clock, but it was many more years before he'd close before that. There was no stopping with Daddy. You had to get the job done. It was work, sleep, work, sleep. He taught us all the hard way, the right way."

"This was Daddy's race team. The one on the left would be Jack Stagner, Bud Stagner's brother; this is my car in the middle—I hadn't started driving it yet. And that's Daddy leaning up against the truck."
BOBBY UNSER
Photo Courtesy of the Unser Family

Fifty-seven years old, Louis awaits his go at Pike's
Peak in 1953, the last year he beat the Mountain.
Photo Courtesy of the Unser Family

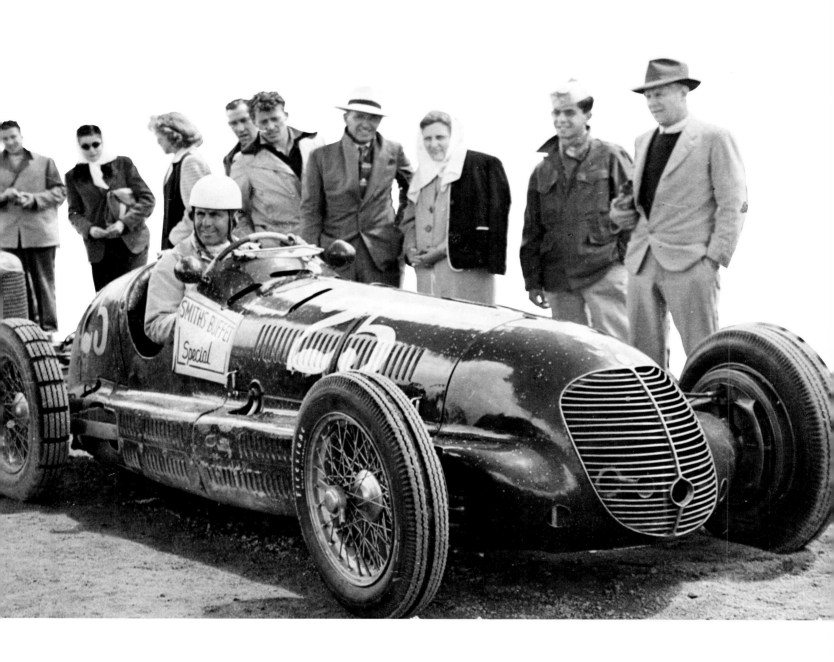

"This is the old house—Mom and Daddy's house—after we put up the wall. That tree is right out behind my garage, still. It really wasn't much. We had a door in the back and that one little section in the back is where we used to sleep—what we called the back porch. We used to take our donkeys in there. I don't know how our mother put up with that."

BOBBY UNSER

Photo Courtesy of the Unser Family

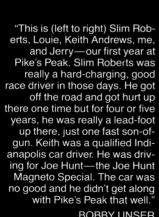

"This is (left to right) Slim Roberts, Louie, Keith Andrews, me, and Jerry—our first year at Pike's Peak. Slim Roberts was really a hard-charging, good race driver in those days. He got off the road and got hurt up there one time but for four or five years, he was really a lead-foot up there, just one fast son-of-gun. Keith was a qualified Indianapolis car driver. He was driving for Joe Hunt—the Joe Hunt Magneto Special. The car was no good and he didn't get along with Pike's Peak that well."

BOBBY UNSER

Photo Courtesy of the Unser Family

Bobby (far right) watches his Uncle Louis attack Pike's
Peak in 1955.

"This is Mom and Daddy in April, 1957. Daddy had arthritic problems. He called it gout, and he did have some gout but it was joint problems. You can see the crutch."

BOBBY UNSER

Photo Courtesy of the Unser Family

The nurturing ground for the Unser talents at various stages of growth.

Photos Courtesy of the Unser Family

For his sons' race cars, Jerry adopted a patriotic red, white and blue color scheme. The boys carried the colors whenever they could for ten or 15 years and on other odd occasions as recently as 1982. If an Unser owned the race car, it was likely to be painted some combination of red, white and blue. "Daddy was always a true-blue American," says Bobby. "He always flew the flag here at the shop and the race cars were always painted red, white and blue." To an Unser, you understand, patriotism is as natural as breathing.

The Unsers soon established themselves as formidable competitors on the local short tracks across New Mexico, into Colorado, Arizona and beyond. Their reputations, however, weren't confined to the on-track activities. The word soon spread: "You don't mess with the Unsers." They might have looked gangly, even a bit scrawny. Maybe, but they soon became equally as well known for the prowess of their fists.

In 1955, Jerry took his three oldest sons to Pike's Peak to challenge both the mountain and Uncle Louis' records and reputation. Each of the boys had his own car, one with a Jaguar engine, one powered by an Oldsmobile, and the third by a 220-cubic inch Offenhauser. They finished third, fourth and fifth that first year. Jerry was pleased with his son's finishes, knowing that they had done their best. However, he was even more pleased with what he had witnessed before the family even left Albuquerque for Colorado. His brother, the boys' Uncle Louis, was the catalyst.

At Indy in 1965, Jerry and Mary gaze proudly at their sons (left to right) Al, Louie and Bobby.
Photo Courtesy of the Unser Family

With son Bobby running Goodyear tires at the Speedway in 1967 and son Al on Firestone, what could Mom and Daddy Unser do but wear the "Fireyear" and "Goodstone" jackets?
Photo Courtesy of the Unser Family

29

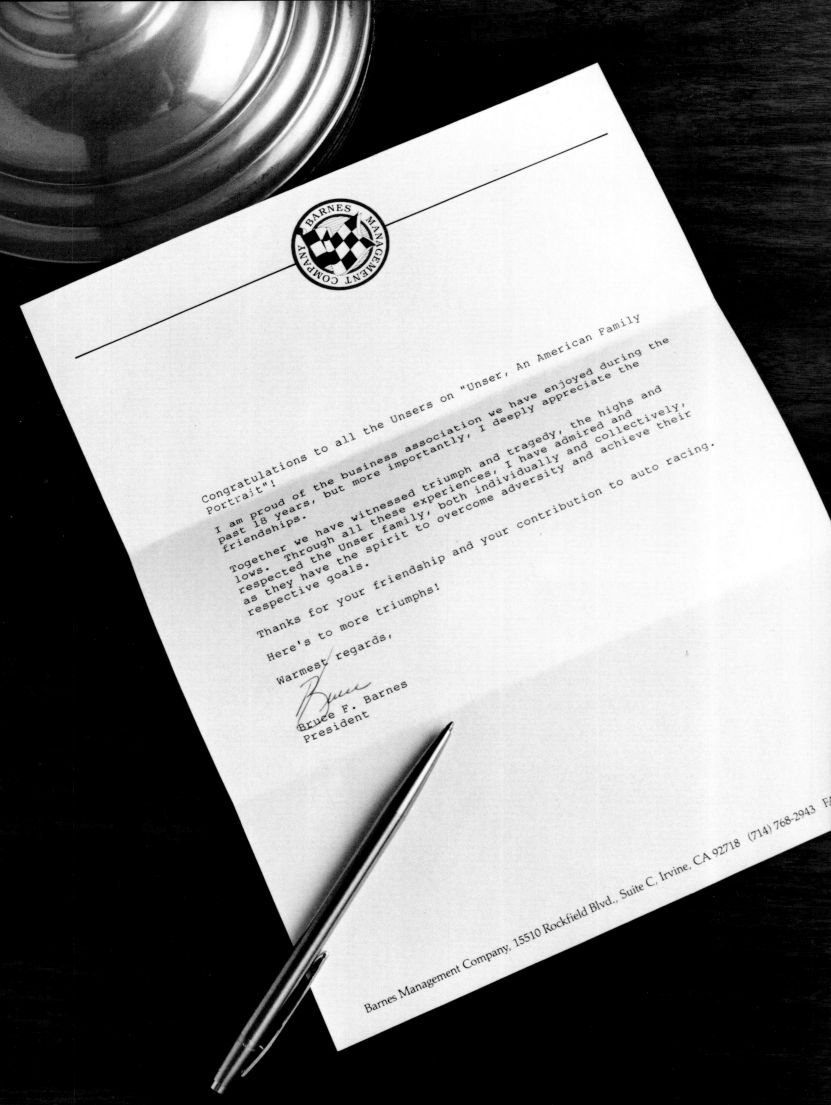

Congratulations to all the Unsers on "Unser, An American Family Portrait"!

I am proud of the business association we have enjoyed during the past 18 years, but more importantly, I deeply appreciate the friendships.

Together we have witnessed triumph and tragedy, the highs and lows. Through all these experiences, I have admired and respected the Unser family, both individually and collectively, as they have the spirit to overcome adversity and achieve their respective goals.

Thanks for your friendship and your contribution to auto racing.

Here's to more triumphs!

Warmest regards,

Bruce

Bruce F. Barnes
President

Barnes Management Company, 15510 Rockfield Blvd., Suite C, Irvine, CA 92718   (714) 768-2943   FA

Louie, Bobby, Mom and Al.
Photo Courtesy of the Unser Family

Uncle Louis was adamant in his belief that Jerry's boys were too young to contest Pike's Peak. If, he felt, Jerry just *had* to let the boys run, then the vehicles should be nothing if not slow. So staunch was Uncle Louis' belief that he persuaded the owner of a high-powered Offy to renege on the ride that had been offered to nephew Louis.

Louis told his brothers and father the sad news while they were gathered, not surprisingly, in the garage. Bobby was aghast, threw a grease rag down and immediately offered his brother the Jaguar he had been building for himself—a car, he swore, which "can outrun any Offy on the Hill." Jerry later reflected on the incident, "I've always taught my kids to be

When Jerome and Marie made that terrifying yet thrilling journey to the United States from their home in Europe, little did they realize how completely their dreams would be fulfilled by their progeny. On January 23, 1986, Jerome and Marie's grandsons, Al and Bobby and their great-grandson, Al Junior, were received by the President of the United States. Left to right: Al and Shelley Unser, Jr.; President Reagan; Al and Karen Unser; Marsha and Bobby Unser.

Photo Courtesy of the Unser Family

Photo by Bill Fitz-Patrick

sportsmanlike and unselfish but this was asking too much of Bobby. That Jag was made for his style of driving and driving it in the race was all he ever dreamed of. I was half choked up, but all I could say was, 'Pick up the grease rag, Bobby.'"

The Unser domination of Pike's Peak began the following year, 1956, when Bobby, driving his Jaguar, scored the first of his 13 wins to date.

"We raced to beat each other and most of all to beat Uncle Louis," says Bobby. "Uncle Louis was always Daddy's biggest competitor so that made Uncle Louis our biggest competitor. That was what got me into racing—not to win the Indianapolis 500 three times but to beat Uncle Louis. That was my whole motivation. I told Uncle Louis I would break all his

records. I was going to be King of the Hill. I was going to beat him head-to-head. I wasn't going to stop until I'd broken all of his records and that's exactly what I did.

"Of course, Uncle Louis and a lot of people who were good at Pike's Peak raced only at the Peak. It was a one-time-a-year thing for them, and we were racing all the time, every weekend and more. We had a new attitude, a new approach. Once we got going and got some money behind us, we really started bringing the times down. When we left the starting line we were sideways and when we got to the top we were still sideways. We used all the road and more, I tell you!"

Congressional Record

United States of America

PROCEEDINGS AND DEBATES OF THE 94th CONGRESS, SECOND SESSION

Vol. 122   WASHINGTON, MONDAY, JANUARY 19, 1976   No. 1

Senate

MARY CATHERINE UNSER

Mr. MONTOYA. Mr. President, on December 18, 1975, a great lady and a beloved citizen of New Mexico, Mary Catherine Unser, died. The people of New Mexico and many other Americans who knew about her outstanding contributions to the world of racing join her family in mourning her loss and remembering her many accomplishments.

Mary Catherine Unser was born in Missouri. She was trained as a professional pianist and graduated with honors from Missouri State University. She gave up her career as a musician to become the wife of Jerry Unser, Sr. and the mother of four boys, Jerry Jr., Louis, Robert, and Al. She left a gentle and protected world to go with her family into the rugged and difficult profession of automobile racing. Bringing with her a marvelous strength and courage, an unending kindness and compassion for people, and the highest possible standards for herself and her family, she adapted quickly to her new career as a member of her husband's racing crew. She learned how to pump gas, keep track of parts, and even how to change a tire in an emergency. She shared the excitement and the hard work with her husband until her boys were old enough to look over the windshield of a racing car. She drove the mechanic's truck during the Mexican road race, and always stood ready to comfort and care for her family of racing men, from Argentina to Canada.

Over the years she came to be known and loved by racing men and women and by fans. The world of "Gasoline Alley," as those who pursue this difficult and dangerous profession call it, soon learned that Mom Unser was friend and inspiration to her own sons and to everyone whose life touched hers.

She gave her family the will to win and pride in their performance. She never tolerated anything but an immaculate appearance for either her family or for their racing cars. She was feminine and gracious and proud.

Her sons Robert and Al won the Indianapolis 500 four times and the national driving championship three times, and I know those honors were important to her. But she was equally proud of their accomplishments as citizens and Americans.

We in New Mexico are happy that she came to our State to make her home. Famous men and women from around the world came to visit her in Albuquerque, and she brought great honor to us there. Her sanctuary was her home in the beautiful city of Chama, N. Mex., where after the racing season she would retire to catch up on her correspondence and to test her world-famous chili recipe.

The world, this Nation, and my State are all better for having known and honored this woman. Her children and grandchildren are carrying on in the Unser traditions which she set. Her race is over, but those of us who knew her will always remember her many victories.

She was always there when the words "gentlemen, start your engines" were called, always with a prayer that none of the drivers would be hurt and a hope that, if the Good Lord were willing, one of her sons would be given the checkered flag.

I know that my colleagues in the Senate and the House of Representatives would want to join me in honoring this fine and brave New Mexican for a race well run.

While Pike's Peak launched the Unsers to auto racing fame, it was the Indianapolis Motor Speedway that caused their names to be written boldly in the history books of the sport. Jerry Junior was the first of the boys to make it to the fabled Speedway. He qualified for the 1958 Indianapolis 500 only to go over the wall in a multi-car accident on the opening lap of the race. The following year on the first day of practice, Jerry crashed and was burned badly. Seventeen days later he died.

Needless to say, Jerry's death did not deter the family's passion for racing. Four years later, brother Bobby qualified for his first of nineteen starts at Indianapolis, and in 1965, younger brother Al made his first start in the 500. Bobby scored the family's first

Coronary Fatal To 'Mom' Unser

Albuquerque, N.M. (UPI) — Mary Unser, the head of one of the best known auto racing families in the country, died yesterday apparently of a heart attack. She was 69.

Mrs. Unser collapsed at her home about noon, said officials at Presbyterian Hospital. She was pronounced dead on arrival at the hospital a short time later of "coronary failure," officials said.

Mrs. Unser was known as 'Mom' to race car drivers and followers because of the racing exploits of her sons — Bobby and Al.

BOBBY UNSER, IN A nearby hospital having a pin removed from his leg when his mother died, won his second Indianapolis 500 title this year. He and Al have won the title in four of the past eight years.

Mrs. Unser, raised at St. Louis, married the late Jerry Unser Sr., at Colorado Springs while on a summer vacation. The family first became known in racing circles by entering, and frequently winning, the annual Pikes Peak auto race at Colorado Springs.

Jerry Unser Sr., died in 1967, the year before Bobby won his first Indy title. A son, Jerry Jr., died in a crash at the Indianapolis Motor Speedway in 1959.

Funeral services for Mrs. Unser are pending.

Indianapolis 500 victory in 1968 with Al winning back-to-back races in 1970 and '71, Bobby winning again in 1975, Al coming home first in '78, Bobby taking his third 500 victory in '81, and Al scoring his fourth win in the race in 1987. Seven times in 20 years the Unser name has been celebrated in Indianapolis' Victory Lane.

Beyond their remarkable success at Indianapolis, Bobby and Al Unser have also shared five national Championships (two for Bobby and three for Al) and are ranked third (Al) and fourth (Bobby) behind only AJ Foyt and Mario Andretti in the all-time listing of Indycar race winners. Since 1983 Al and his son Al Junior have raced each other as well as the rest of the field at Indianapolis and elsewhere. And, in 1985, father and son engaged in a memorable duel for the national Championship down to the last lap of the last race of the year.

Jerry Junior's twin brother Louie wasn't quite as successful a driver as his two younger brothers, although he twice won the stock car class at Pike's Peak. He was chief mechanic for both Jerry Junior's and Al's first Indy 500 experiences, a setting in which his gifts sparkled. Louis left Albuquerque for California, changed the spelling of his name to Louie, and created an enviable reputation as a race car and race boat engine builder. Struck by Multiple Sclerosis in 1964, Louie retired from driving but continues, iron-willed, to run his engine-building business.

The texture and style of the Unser family's assault on automobile racing's record books was established, of course, by Jerry and Mary Unser. He with his restless spirit and granite-like persistence, she with a deep love for family and home. Together, Jerry and Mary Unser provided their sons with a perfectly natural framework to pursue their lives as race car drivers. As the boys became successful at the family's chosen trade, Mom and Daddy Unser continued to support them, going to the races, cheering for them from the pits. The parents became as familiar to race-goers as the race-winning Unser brothers, and Mary's chili cook-outs with sons assisting were enjoyable, garage-side social occasions at a number of national Championship races in the early and mid-seventies. Jerry died on September 14, 1967. Mary continued to provide her sons and their families with the support and encouragement on which they thrived until her death on December 17, 1975, at age 68. To this day, the dynasty Jerry and Mary Unser helped create continues to grow—winning races and setting records. Few people in the history of automobile racing can lay claim to such a legacy.

Jerry Unser, Jr. ready to take on the Indianapolis 500 his rookie year.

The Twins, Jerry & Louie

erry and Mary's firstborn were a pair of twin boys born ten minutes apart, Jerry Junior, the eldest, and Louis. Although both were driven by the Unser spirit, the twins were physically and mentally dissimilar. Jerry was taller, stronger, successful in sports, popular with the girls. Louis was comparatively scrawny. He was light-haired, talked with a stutter and was a tough little scrapper of a kid. Louis felt always that he was the black sheep of the family, ultimately changing the spelling of his name to Louie. In Louie's view, nothing he could do was good enough.

In high school, Jerry was the star of the wrestling team. It was rare that he lost a single match. "Jerry was a fanatic about wrestling," says Bobby. "He was an exceptionally strong person. He didn't look that big but nobody could whip him. Jerry used to just play with guys who had huge muscles. Even a guy like Foyt who is a bull of a man—very strong. Jerry could've whipped Foyt. When we were on the wrestling team in high school, I used to win about 80 percent of my matches, but Jerry would win 100 percent of his matches."

Unlike his twin, Louie didn't join the high school wrestling team. "I was always in detention," says Louie. "I guess I was the wildest of Jerry, Bobby, and me. Daddy and I were too much alike. We fought. He was hard-headed and I'm hard-headed. Good thing too or else I wouldn't still be going or have the memories I have. When we were teenagers in Albuquerque and were out somewhere and somebody would start talking to Bobby's girlfriend, Bobby would say, 'Let's go over and kick the hell out of that guy.' And I'd go over and do it. Sometimes it would take 15 minutes 'cause I wasn't very big but usually, I'd get it done. Sometimes they'd kick the hell out of me. Whatever Jerry or Bobby or even Al wanted, I was ready to make sure it would happen.

"I used to stutter real bad when I was a kid. When I was in the service, through most of my life, I couldn't talk. I stuttered so bad I couldn't say, 'Good morning.' I couldn't even say my name. I couldn't say Albuquerque. Instead of talking to somebody, I'd just bust 'em. That way I didn't have to talk, didn't have to argue. I'd put 'em on their asses. Then I would end up in jail and Daddy would have to come and get me out."

When the boys started racing, they took their aggressive style with them to the racetracks. "Several times we had to back out of a racetrack," says Louie, "because we were fighting. There were a couple of times when Bobby had won the race, blowed their tails off—and there was enough aggravation that we got to fighting and had to leave before the police arrived."

Nevertheless, the Unsers quickly proved themselves to be very fast, competitive drivers. Both Jerry Junior and Louie won races.

39

Seven-year-old Louie (left) and Jerry in front of Daddy's filling station.
Photo Courtesy of the Unser Family

Jerry and Louie at the toddler stage.
Photo Courtesy of the Unser Family

Jerry (right) and Louie are dwarfed by a team of Clydesdales.
Photo Courtesy of the Unser Family

JERRY JUNIOR.
Photo Courtesy of the Unser Family

School Days
1941-42

LOUIE.
Photo Courtesy of the Unser Family

School Days
1941-42

In September of '52 oldest brother Jerry, having joined the Navy, was stationed in Hawaii. Through both his driving and his dedication, he made the Unser name famous in the Pacific Islands. Driving a '31 Chevy coupe powered by a GMC truck engine, Jerry won the Hawaiian stock car title in 1953 and was runner-up in '54, winning every feature race he finished that year. The quickly growing legend was further fueled when fans discovered that not only was Jerry winning—he was winning with a broken arm. Before leaving the Naval base, Jerry would slit his cast open, go race (and win), return to the base, replace the cast, replaster the slit and wait until the next event. Jerry was an overnight sensation in

Hawaii and was flown by both track promoters and the Navy from island to island. When he went home at the end of 1954, he was sent on his way by a gala "Jerry Unser Aloha Night."

As their reputations grew, Jerry Senior got ready to introduce his three oldest sons to Pike's Peak. Jerry and Louie approached their debut as they approached life— with different styles. As Jerry Junior labored in his father's garage, building a car with which to challenge The Hill, Louie arranged to drive someone else's car. Intensely aware of his uncle's accomplishments and position in the family, young Louie set about learning the mountain road by driving a tour bus up the mountain during the summer of '54.

"When you got to running in a race car," says Louie, "it looked a whole lot different than it did from the bus! But it helped. At least I knew which way the road went."

Jerry (left) commemorates a memorable day in May, 1952 with Navy buddies Billy Elko and Bill Sieger.
Photo Courtesy of the Unser Family

Jerry and long-time sweetheart Betty Jo Herring.
Photo Courtesy of the Unser Family

Jerry demonstrates his prodigious strength.
Photo Courtesy of the Unser Family

Jerry and his 1931 Chevrolet Coupe with the GMC
truck engine became the toast of Hawaii.

Jerry finished his maiden Pike's Peak competition in fourth place, driving an Offenhauser-powered racer. Louie finished in third—but not in the ride he had intended. Uncle Louis' belief that all his nephews were too young to drive a powerful car had convinced Louie's car owner to back out of the deal. Bobby rescued his brother's dream by relinquishing his own car, a Jaguar, so that Louie might compete. Many observers thought Louie would have won had his brake handle not broken. "There was no doubt about it," declares Bobby. "Louie would have won, but at the 16-mile mark (three miles from the finish line) his brake handle broke."

It was at this time that Louie was making the decision to get out of Albuquerque. "I was always in trouble with somebody in Albuquerque," says Louie, "I was in trouble there all my life, on my own and with Bobby.

"There were times when I filled in for Bobby when he was in the Army and away racing. One time in Cheyenne I was dressed in Bobby's fatigues on the base. We were in the chow hall and a lieutenant came in. Everybody but me saluted. I forgot you had to do that. The sergeant said to me, 'Hey Unser, don't you respect the rank of a Lieutenant?' 'I'm sorry sir,' I said. I told him I hadn't recognized the lieutenant. Then the lieutenant walked over and looked at my name on my fatigues and told me to come and see him in his office the next morning. Now that was a tough one to get out of … anyway, I just got in enough trouble on my own and with Bobby that I decided it was time to leave Albuquerque."

While racing in Hawaii, if Jerry didn't win there was usually ample evidence as to what prevented a trip to victory circle.
Photo Courtesy of the Unser Family

43

Hawaii Loses Sports Idol As Unser Returns Here

By H. F. MULLEN
Journal Sports Writer

Hawaii lost one of its idols recently, and it wasn't one of the stone-and-ceramic kind.

The object that has drawn the worship of sports fans there for the past two years is a 22-year-old modified-stock car driver from Albuquerque named Jerry Unser Jr.

To a resident of the mainland, it is surprising that a relatively new and minor sport such as auto racing would produce a national hero—but in the islands, racing is king. Baseball, football, and other mass spectacles run second to the roar of the jalopies.

As to the part that Jerry Unser played in this craze, first let it be said that he is the son of Mr. and Mrs. Unser, 7700 Central Ave. West and was discharged this spring from the Navy.

He was assigned by the Navy to Hawaii in Sept. 1952 after having raced here for two years. In 1953, he won the Hawaiian stock car racing championship, competing three or four nights a week on the various islands there that have tracks. Promoters soon found it profitable to fly the likeable kid from one island to another as his popularity increased.

His racing car, a 1931 Chevrolet coupe with a GMC truck engine, was transported by barge.

The average field of cars at the big track in Honolulu is 125 cars and only the top 24 are entered in the feature race. The oval is inside a football stadium that seats 28,000, and on four occasions the place has been packed and fans turned away during the 10-month season.

Jerry figures he won about $10,000 during his two-year stay, with "most of it going back into the car." Unser developed a style of driving that was particularly pleasing to the Hawaiians. He was reported as an unusually "clean" driver but he kept the fans howling with his "go for broke" style. Unser explains that this simply means not being content to hold third or fourth place near the end of a race—but to gamble on skidding off the track in last-minute attempts to pass the leaders and take first place.

In 1954, Unser was runnerup in point standings, finishing second by 11 points. However, he won every main event he raced, with the exception of those in which his "go for broke" policy put him out of the event with mechanical trouble or a collision.

But the real story of Unser's stay in Hawaii is not the races he won.

It's the almost believable hero worship that was bestowed upon the 22-year-old Albuquerquean. Numerous Jerry Unser fan clubs cheered him on the track, and mobbed him in the pits for autographs. For the past two years, Hawaiian newspapers have referred to him as "the favorite of the kids," "the island's sports hero," and "the greatest

racing personality to ever hit the islands."

In a popularity contest among the 125 drivers, Unser led with 283 points, almost as many points as the other 124 entries had received among them. The prize for the contest was a new Chevrolet.

Prior to Jerry's leaving the islands early this year, the staffs of Honolulu's four television stations, two newspapers and several radio stations staged a testimonial dinner for him.

Full-page advertisements ran in the papers announcing "Jerry Unser Aloha Night." Merchants contributed farewell gifts to the promotion and fan clubs went into mourning.

Twenty thousand Hawaiians turned out for the final Aloha day, which included a special match race between Unser and his chief racing competitor. People openly wept in the grandstands when a good-luck telegram from Mr. and Mrs. Unser was read over the public address system during intermission.

Unser set a new 10-lap track record that day as he won the match race, won the heat race, and then lapped the field in the 40-lap main event, finishing almost another lap ahead of the second-place car.

He holds three track records at the Hawaiian oval, and a permanent Jerry Unser Memorial Trophy has been established for the future driver who breaks the 40-lap track record three times in a row.

Jerry is back in Albuquerque now, working in his dad's garage on West Central. His future plans? Big car racing on

the national AAA circuit with a seat someday behind the wheel in the Indianapolis "500."

BEDECKED WITH LEIS: Jerry Unser of Albuquerque received leis of flowers from admiring fans when he concluded his two-year auto racing career in Hawaii while stationed there with the Navy. Twenty thousand fans turned out for the "Jerry Unser Aloha Day" to bid farewell to islands' sports hero. The youngster at right, Davey Cook, is a member of the Jerry Unser fan club and wears a racing jacket identical to his ideal.

BEAUTY IS MORE THAN SKIN DEEP.

All of us at Newell Coach salute the Unsers.
America's grand family of racing.

Louie went to southern California and began working as a race car mechanic and engine-builder. He continued to run as a team with brother Jerry, however, and over the next few years Jerry and Louie built one of the strongest stock car teams of the times. In 1956, Jerry won the newly-revised stock car class at Pike's Peak. In 1957, he not only again won the stock car class, but he and Louie also combined to win that year's USAC's national stock car title.

"Jerry and I went back east that year with two cars," says Louie. "But there was just the two of us working on the cars and it was taking 20 hours a day just to get one car running right. So we decided that instead of running two cars half-assed, we would run one car for Jerry and win the Championship. I knew Jerry could do it. So that's what we did. We ran one car and Jerry drove. In two races we ran Bobby in the second car to help Jerry in the points. We won the Championship out here at Riverside." To this day, Louie proudly wears the national Championship ring won that year by him and his twin brother.

In 1958, Jerry went to Indianapolis for the first time. He and Louie went as a team—driver and chief mechanic. After jumping from car to car, Jerry finally qualified for that year's race only to be eliminated in a multi-car, first lap accident. As eight cars were knocked-out of the race in the third turn incident, Jerry's car went over the wall. He was lucky to escape with a dislocated shoulder; popular veteran Pat O'Connor was killed in the accident.

Louie spent much of 1954 driving a Pike's Peak tour bus in order to learn which way the road up the mountain went.

Photo Courtesy of the Unser Family

Louie ready to tackle Pike's Peak in 1955.
Photo Courtesy of the Unser Family

Jerry ready to go at Pike's Peak.
Photo Courtesy of the Unser Family

47

Jerry charges across the Pike's
Peak finish line.
Photo Courtesy of the Unser Family

Driving the Jaguar that Bobby had originally built for his own effort, Louie makes his maiden assault on Pike's Peak.
Photo Courtesy of the Unser Family

Jerry drove his Cady L. Daniels Chevrolet to the 1956 stock car class win at Pike's Peak in 1956.
Photo Courtesy of the Unser Family

Louie tackled Pike's Peak in 1956 behind the wheel of a stretched Midget powered by a super-charged Offy.
Photo Courtesy of the Unser Family

Photo by Stewart's

Photo by Stewart's

"The first car Jerry drove at the Speedway that year was much too slow," says Louie. "So we found another ride at Sumar Racing but a bird was sucked through the engine. I tried to rebuild the engine but we couldn't get some parts and Jerry was out shopping for rides. He got into a car that Don Edmunds had crashed. They rebuilt the car and Edmunds tried again but he couldn't get it up to speed. So Jerry took it over, went out and ran it. The handling wasn't right so we worked on it and Jerry got it up to speed, qualified for the race. We went out and got some of our own people to run the car in the race. I didn't go to bed for three or four nights. We rebuilt everything on that car. Then, in the race, of course, Pat O'Connor and Pat Flaherty got together and Jerry went over the wall."

The following year Jerry got a ride in a competitive car. Louie wasn't part of the team but he planned to be there to give his brother advice and whatever help might be needed. "I got married to Marty in Albuquerque right before practice began at Indy that year," recounts Louie. "I told Jerry on the phone not to go out 'til I got there. I told him I'd be there on Monday but on Saturday, he went out on a set of experimental tires. He hit the wall, crashed and burned.

Left

Jerry (#172) finds his Mickey Thompson Special flanked by Dan Gurney (#69) in a Ferrari Testa Rosa prior to the 1956 running of the Pomona Grand Prix.

Photo Courtesy of the Unser Family

Right

Louie leads Bobby around the Arizona State Fairgrounds.

Photo Courtesy of the Unser Family

50

Left

Louie goes hillclimbing at Pike's Peak in 1957.

Photo Courtesy of the Unser Family

Right

Jerry won Pike's Peak stock car class for the second consecutive year in 1957.

Photo Courtesy of the Unser Family

Bobby (right) and Louie take a break during a car e
Photo Courtesy of the Unser

"The funny part to it is that same day they put me into the hospital in Albuquerque. I felt so bad I thought I was going to die, but they couldn't find anything wrong with me. I checked myself out that night and went home. The next day I found out Jerry had hit the wall. With Jerry and me, he could have been 3,000 miles away and if something happened, I could sense it. We were twins, you know."

Jerry was burned very badly and finally, 17 days after the accident, a combination of the burn damage and pneumonia took his life. "He had what they call third degree burns," says Louie, "But really, they don't have a number to describe how bad he was burned over his back and legs and kidneys."

Louie was deeply affected by the loss of his favorite brother, his twin. He returned to his adopted home in California and ran some Sprint and stock car races. "I ran some races but I wasn't happy doing it. I quit for a while. I was sure I would never do it again. But that only lasted for two or three

The 1957 USAC national stock car Champion receives congratulations at Riverside.
Photo Courtesy of the Unser Family

Photo by Lester Nehamkin

months, because time heals everything. It ended up that I wasn't happy with what I was doing. I wasn't racing so I went back to it."

In 1960 and '61 Louie came back with a vengeance, winning the stock car class both years at Pike's Peak. Setting records both years, in 1960 he broke his brother Jerry's record set in 1958. Driving at Pike's Peak, Louie was extremely aggressive. Many veterans say a conservative style is best—safest at a place like Pike's Peak where a mistake can spell big trouble. Says Louie: "I drove super hot, it's true. I guarantee you that if I got to the top I would win. A few times I didn't get to the top but when I made it with a healthy car, I usually won."

Although he proved himself as good a driver as his brothers, Louie was in demand as a mechanic and tuner. In 1963 and '64 he worked on Ford's AC Cobra sports car team. He was also employed by a number of other Detroit manufacturers to do developmental and experimental work. Then, late in 1964, he learned he had been stricken with multiple sclerosis.

"This was at Speedway Park here in Albuquerque. Jerry was doing a demonstration run for the local fans. He had just become national (USAC stock car) Champion. Jerry was really the first really big thing to come out of Albuquerque. I mean, he was the *national* Champion.

"This is (left to right) me, Jerry, Louie, Al, and Daddy."

BOBBY UNSER

Photo Courtesy of the Unser Family

"I went to Africa for the African Safari rally in 1964," says Louie, "and we were there for four months. That's when it first hit me. I came back from Africa and went with Ford on the Cape Horn-to-Fairbanks durability run. I had it then and I knew it. I kept it a secret for a while. I could walk far enough to keep it a secret for a while but I would get very tired. …

"When the doctor told me that I had MS, I said, 'What the hell is that?' I said, 'Give me a shot and lets get rid of it.' He said, 'No, it doesn't work that way.' He told me to slow down to one or two hours a day or else I would kill myself. Well, I'd always worked 16 hours a day, every day of the week, so I just kept going. I was going to let them know I was here before I went. And I'm still doing it. It takes longer. It's a little harder but with the right help, you can get anything done."

Jerry is interviewed by Bob Russo at Indy.
Photo Courtesy of the Unser Family

"This was a Sprint car accident I (#28) had in California. You can see by looking I was lucky to get away that light. I was knocked unconscious but all I ended up with was a sprained neck."
LOUIE UNSER
Photo Courtesy of the Unser Family

A battered Jerry props up his young son following his roll-over at Pike's Peak—or perhaps it's the son doing the propping . . .

Photo Courtesy of the Unser Family

Involved in a massive first-lap incident during the '58 running of the Indy 500, Jerry is knocked not only out of the race but out of the Speedway.

Photos Courtesy of the Unser Family

"This is Jerry's crash at Pike's Peak. It was right after he went over the wall at Indianapolis. The roof was smashed in and came down on top of the steering wheel. It broke his nose. It tore the shit out of that car—tweaked the frame. It rolled up the embankment and then rolled back down again. Jerry had a dislocated shoulder from his accident at Indy so was driving with one hand, shifting and turning with one hand."

LOUIE UNSER

Photos Courtesy of the Unser Family

Louie on his way to the 1961 Pike's Peak stock car class victory.

Louie (#62) races a Midget at Ascot.
Photo Courtesy of the Unser Family

Jerry checks out his cockpit during the running of Pomona's Examiner Grand Prix in March, 1959.

Photo by Bob Tronolone

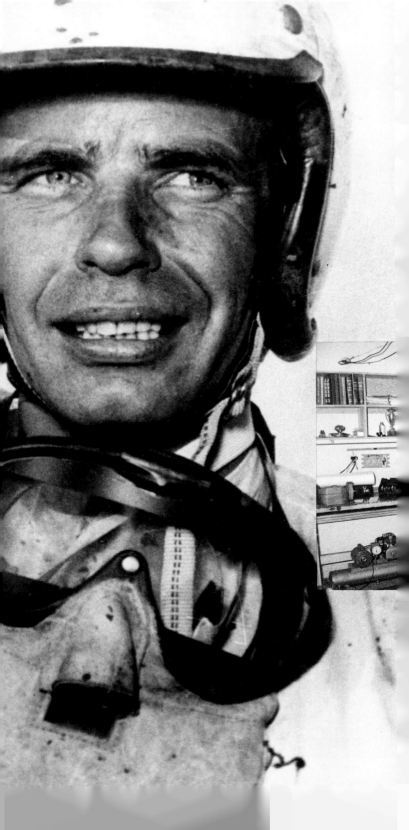

The Unser clan gathers around Louie after his '61 Pike's Peak victory: (back row, left to right) Bobby and (first wife) Barbara; Jeanne (Jerry's widow); Mom and Daddy; Al; (front row, right to left) Wanda (Al's first wife), Marty (Louie's second wife); Louie and daughter Adele.

Photo Courtesy of the Unser Family

Louie contests the USAC 200 at Riverside in 1962.

After the onset of MS forced Louie to retire from working on race cars and race teams, he concentrated on building up his engine business. Wheelchair-bound or not, he was able to build race-winning engines for power boats, off-road cars, speedway motorcycles and other types of racing machines. Louie's engines have become highly-rated in all quarters of the racing business, and Louie continues to work every day at his shop.

Before he was compelled to pull back from his role as a race team crew chief, Louie insisted, in the winter of 1964-'65, on taking one final shot at Indianapolis. His goal was to build a car in which brother Al could take his rookie run at the Speedway. With sponsorship from Frank Arciero and engineering by Pete Weismann, Louie built a Maserati-powered racer. "Starting in November of '64, I worked on that car 20 hours a day, seven days a week. I built it out here in Garden Grove. It was my last chance at the Speedway. I knew it and I put everything into that car."

The car just didn't have the horsepower to be competitive, however. After two weeks of trying to get up to speed, the engine

"This was Dave McDonald's Cobra at Riverside in '63 or '64. He just hit the fence while practicing. I was in charge of Shelby's Cobra program for a couple years."
LOUIE UNSER.

In 1964, Louie Unser challenges Pike's Peak for the last time.

blew apart. It was the last day of qualifying and both Louie and Al were miserably depressed when AJ Foyt surprised them, offering Al his spare car. Al jumped at the chance, and with Louie and Foyt running the car, Louie's baby brother made the race. "Then we got our stuff together and went out and ran the race the next week," adds Louie. "And Al brought it home in ninth place, ran all day. It was a good race for him, a good start for him at the Speedway. I'm glad I was there to be part of it."

Six years after the emotional see-saw of Al's rookie year at Indy, Al's first wife, Wanda, introduced Louie to LaVerne Drabeck. Before the year was out, they were married. Thirty-year-old LaVerne worked as a school teacher in San Diego at the time and had never been married. Louie, on the other hand, had been married twice. He was first married to Bonnie with whom, in 1955, he had a son Jeff, and then to Marty with whom he adopted a daughter, Adele, in 1959. Marty committed suicide ten years later.

When he and LaVerne met, Louie was already living most of his life in a wheelchair. Three years after their marriage LaVerne gave birth to a daughter, Lynn. The family has lived since then in suburban Anaheim, California, a ten-minute drive from Louie's shop in Fullerton. Louie says, "Without LaVerne I wouldn't be able to get out or go to work. She drives me everywhere and makes everything happen for me." An attractive, red-headed woman, LaVerne is devoted to Louie. "He's a very honest man, very willing to help other people," says LaVerne. "He has a very big heart."

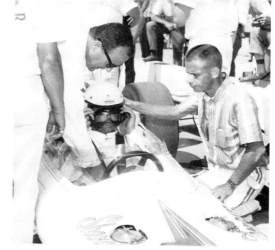

AJ Foyt is showing Al the controls of Foyt's backup Lola in which Al is about to try to qualify for the '65 Indy. Louie (on his knees) listens intently.

As Bobby watches (checked shirt on the left), Louie, Foyt and George Bignotti (right) try unsuccessfully to start the engine.

Foyt continues to labor as Steward Harlen Fengler informs Al that he won't be allowed to qualify.

All work on the car stops as Louie, Bobby and Foyt inform Fengler what he can do with the decision to prevent Al from qualifying.

Al qualified and made the race.

Photos Courtesy of the Unser Family

63

For years Louie and LaVerne have given their time to attending fund-raising dinners and functions for the MS Society and many other charitable institutions. After more than 25 years of fighting a debilitating disease like multiple sclerosis, Louie's spirit of determination and zest for life provide a fine example for other physically handicapped people. In recognition of his accomplishments in life and his efforts to help others, Louie was inducted into Orange County's Hall of Fame in February, 1987.

"I notice, year from year, that I'm getting worse," reflects Louie. "I know that. It's the way it is. My brother Al once asked me, 'How do you do it Louie? How do you keep going?' Well, I guess it's because I want to keep going, to live, to enjoy my family and people. That's what does it."

Louie and LaVerne become husband and wife.
Photo Courtesy of the Unser Family

Louie, LaVerne and daught
Lynn at Ontario Mot
Speedwa
Photo Courtesy of the Unser Fan

64

Photo by Tim Dolan

Louie stops in front of his right-eously famous engine shop.
Photo Courtesy of the Unser Family

Indianapolis, 1981.

Photo by James Cutler

Bobby Unser

Driving the Audi Quattro, Bobby captured the Pike's Peak victor's laurels for the 13th time.

Photo by David Hutson

In 1968, Bobby put his Jud Phillips-prepared Rislone racer in the third spot on the Indianapolis 500 grid with a qualifying speed of 169.507 MPH.

Photo by Bob Tronolone

On the Indycar circuit, any old-timer worth his salt has a Bobby Unser story or two to tell and an attempt at an impersonation. Inevitably, an impersonator will try to emulate the classic Bobby Unser punch line. It's a crisply delivered closing phrase: "I'm tellin' you, son!" Done correctly, the impersonation will be characterized by an awful mocking of anything less than total belief in both the anecdote and in the lessons inherent in the tale because Bobby is that kind of man. He is larger than life, a real character, impassioned, obstinate.

Before the 48-year-old Unser retired, with great reluctance, from driving Indycars at the end of 1982, Bobby had enshrined himself in the annals of American automobile racing in unique fashion. On the record and in the memory of those who saw him race, he stands as one of the hardest, most persistent old salts ever to sit in a race car. His driving career spanned 33 years, and he won races in almost every conceivable type of car. But it was Bobby's uncompromisingly aggressive method of going about the business of racing automobiles that stands him on his own historical turf.

Bobby considers himself a man who made himself into a successful race car driver by force of will. He is adamant that a burning desire to master the family skills of mechanics and driving overcame any shortages he may

have possessed in family money or physical capabilities: timing, reactions, eyesight, and the dynamic sensitivity that must be part of any race driver's physiological composition. Bobby defers readily to his younger brother, Al, and nephew, Al Junior, when the talk turns to "natural talent," but he'll always make the point that the desire to succeed, the commitment—"total commitment," in his words—is still the most important factor in the arcane, complex world of automobile racing.

Bobby was always entirely consumed by racing, often pushing himself and the people around him to the breaking point. When he finally retired from Indycar competition, he doubted his decision. He doubted his ability to live without fast cars and the intensive effort required to make them even faster. "Even though I have retired," he said at the time, "my subconscious mind hasn't quit. It's still racing. It's like a racing machine. *I'm* like a racing machine. And it's very hard to turn it off.

"Somehow-or-other," he continued, "I've got to convince myself I'm not Bobby Unser the Indianapolis race car driver, anymore. I've made up my mind to retire from Indycars, and now I've got to convince my subconscious that this is the way it is.

"You have to realize how much time I've always spent on racing. I have a problem in that I usually work too hard and before you know it, it's a 110 percent deal. So now I have to find out: Am I going to become a frustrated person? Am I going to find new interests? It's obvious that I can't become a vacation person. Four days of vacation time and I'm a basket case. That's just the way I am."

■ *"Back in the early days, Pike's Peak was literally my grubstake. In 1959 I ran my own car for the first time and that was also the year I bought my first airplane, a Cessna 170B with a tired engine that I paid $3,200 for. I used that plane to fly to races in California and I remember going into Pike's Peak that year with my own car — I was broke. There was a lot of money to win back then—$5,000—which was a lot of money in those days. Between my wife and me, we had about one dollar, and if the car had broken on the way up I would not have been able to pay back all the people I owed for parts that were in the car. I wouldn't have been able to pay our hotel bill. I wouldn't have been able to pay any of the bills waiting at home. I don't know what I would have done. But the car held together, and I won the race, set a new record as well."*

69

"This is me standing on top of my donkey. All of us boys had our donkeys. That's Jerry's standing over there on the right. His name was Silver. This one's (Bobby's) Star. This is right in the back yard."

BOBBY UNSER

Photo Courtesy of the Unser Family

School Days
1941-42

"This in 1952, in high school, when I was on the wrestling team. That's the Boys' Ranch, in Texas. I won by a pin.

"I enjoyed wrestling more than anything—it was Olympic-type wrestling, not like you see on television. It's the hardest sport, for being in shape, that there is. You have to train, I guess, twice as much as a football player. For working out, wrestling is the hardest, harder than boxing, harder than track. We had to pump weights, plus run, plus do push-ups, we had to do everything, and bunches of it."

BOBBY UNSER

Photo Courtesy of the Unser Family

"This is the wrestling team and that's me (third from left) and that's Jerry (second from left). Jerry was also on the wrestling team and Jerry was the best. Jerry was a coordinated athlete and exceptionally strong. Jerry was by far the strongest. There wasn't anybody in high school he couldn't whip—there wasn't anybody. I don't care who he was or where he come from; how mean he was, how big he was; how good a boxer, whatever. Jerry was just a natural athlete: a good, coordinated, strong person."

BOBBY UNSER

Photo Courtesy of the Unser Family

Indeed. In his racing days Bobby was always fiddling: adjusting the set-up of his car's chassis, engine, transmission, or aerodynamics. He grew up building and working on the cars he raced and always played a large hand in the type and direction of the technical changes and development of his cars. To each team for which he drove, he brought a wealth of knowledge and opinion garnered through hands-on experience—a contribution which at times was difficult for non-believers to accept.

"This would have been the Chrysler-engined Super Modified car. It was my third race car. That was one of those cars that was just awesome. I just won all the races. Just won. Almost everything we did in Albuquerque, I just won a lot of races. My Dad *always* had good cars for me."

BOBBY UNSER
Photo Courtesy of the Unser Family

Photo by Hassebrach

"Oh, yea. That's Tommy Drisdale. He was the most fantastic Midget race driver. He was one of the coldest, hardest people that I ever knew in my life. And yet, to me, he was a very good supporter. That guy would do something *mean* to somebody in a Midget. He'd 'park' a guy—what we used to call, "Parkin' 'em." He'd get a guy on his head, or put a guy into the fence, or something. I mean, just one of the meanest guys I ever knew. And yet, one of the nicest guys I ever knew. He just really took a liking to me.

"I started racing in '49 so I'm only like 16 years old here. And, I'd just won a big race, whatever. Both of these trophies would be mine. And I'm bald! I just got shaved in high school. I'm trying to think, there was some club that I belonged to in high school. It's the only year I went to high school. I didn't finish high school. I just had joined the club, and I was too embarrassed to go out there, so I put a hat on my head. Because they absolutely shaved you, right down to a bald head."

BOBBY UNSER

Photo Courtesy of the Unser Family

"This is the Jaguar that my dad and I drove in the first Mexican road race. We ran a Jaguar the first year, a Chrysler the second year."

BOBBY UNSER

Photo Courtesy of the Unser Family

"This is me standing along side the '31 Pontiac my dad gave us for Christmas one time and then he and I made a race car out of it. It must have been in 1951. It was my second Super Modified."

BOBBY UNSER

Photo Courtesy of the Unser Family

"This was the second year (of participating in the Mexican Road Race), 1952. Daddy's on the right and I'm on the left. Daddy would drive around the first corner and then we'd switch."

BOBBY UNSER

Photo Courtesy of the Unser Family

Living Legends Ride
ski-doo®

When the Unsers... the world's
No. 1 Indy-car racing family...
hit the snow, they ride Ski-Doo,
the world's premier snowmobile.
Living legends don't settle for
anything but the best.

Al Unser Jr.　　*Bobby Unser*　　*Al Unser*

 *Better ideas make better snowmobiles*

"This was really a neat day. This was in 1981 at Riverside. It was the father/son race, and we all used equal Toyotas. Toyota put the thing on, and they took the fathers and sons like Mario and Michael, Al and Al Junior, Jack Brabham and his son Geoff, Willy Ribbs and his father. And Bobby Junior and I ran first and second! He led most of the race, and I ended up passing him right at the latter part, and I got first and he got second and Uncle Al was third and Little Al was fifth. That was a good race.

"Bobby had just finished the Bondurant driving school a week before that. And came down there and we just kicked everybody's rear end."

BOBBY UNSER

"Yeah, we qualified first and second and finished first and second. We started inverted. Remember, they put us in the last row."

BOBBY UNSER, JR.

Photo Courtesy of the Unser Family

Mementos of the Unser's second Mexican Road Race adorn the wall in Bobby's Albuquerque home.

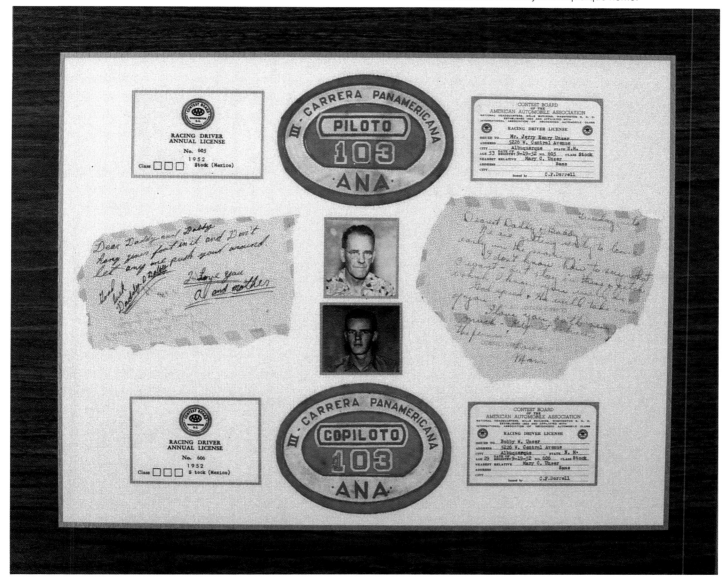

The Jaguar-powered Super Modified campaigned by Bobby in 1954.

Photo Courtesy of the Unser Family

"This was 1954 and the Jaguar, and I probably won the race that night. It was a Super Modified race in Albuquerque."

BOBBY UNSER

Photo Courtesy of the Unser Family

"You're in the Air Force now", Airman Bobby Unser.

"A guy named Ken Bradley who was in the service with me had a Plymouth and I had been reading that these Plymouths were fast cars. So I talked him into running his car in a 500 lap race out at Speedway Park. There wasn't a roll bar or anything else in that car. It was literally, totally, off the street. It was his wife's car and she was a German girl who ran the family with a hammer. He told her I was fixing his car in the garage and we stripped it down. We took the grille out, took the things off that we thought might get broken. Daddy got a bigger radiator from somewhere and we put that in because we were afraid it might overheat. Then we took it out to Speedway Park and we won the race!

"Now, that's only part of it because during the race I'm looking up in the grandstands and there's hardly anybody there. So I knew that something terrible was happening. I didn't trust the promoter and I figured something was wrong so when I took the checkered flag I ran right on through the gate. I drove right on up to the pay shack and caught the promoter coming out the door! He had a bag with all the money and I grabbed him and put the bag on the hood of the car. We split up the money among everybody and then took the Plymouth I'd been driving back to the garage, put the hubcaps and grille back on, left the radiator in it, cleaned it, rolled the windows back up and gave it back to his wife. And she never would have known the difference.

"So this is Ken Bradley (left) and his baby and wife and Bob Cropper (right). Mrs. Bradley obviously knew about her car after the deal."

BOBBY UNSER

Photo Courtesy of the Unser Family

"This is 1955, the house I used to live in. I put a little bit of an addition on the back. You see that color change? That cost me $1500 bucks. No sidewalk ... I lived there two or three years. Man-oh-man-oh-man, there wasn't anything out there in those days, I mean nothing! We used to raise centipedes and black widows in that house. That's where Bobby Junior and Cindy lived when they were born.

"When the sand would blow really bad, sometimes we would just open the doors and let it blow on through."

BOBBY UNSER

Photo Courtesy of the Unser Family

"This is in 1955. This was my Super Modified. Then we took this body off and made a Pike's Peak car out of it and called it the 'Ugly Duckling.' The Foutz brothers (the Super Modified sponsor) struck uranium and just became instant millionaires."

BOBBY UNSER

Photo Courtesy of the Unser Family

Bobby and his father pose by the "Ugly Duckling."

Photo Courtesy of the Unser Family

At various stages of his career (with All-American Racers in 1971-75 and Penske Racing from 1979-81), Bobby was clearly the man to beat in Indycar racing, a frequent fast qualifier and race leader. Awesome as his dominance was on those occasions, he probably won fewer races than he should have due to some kind of mechanical or tactical failure—often as a direct result of Bobby's eternal searching for more speed, a greater technical advantage.

Consumed by a desire to dominate, he leaned hard on people, demanding no less than what he was willing to give—a situation which could inspire only intense loyalty or equally intense dislike.

Twice he left Dan Gurney's All-American Racers: the first time at the end of 1975 and again in 1978 after a brief renewal of acquaintances. Today, the mention of Bobby's name can bring a scowl from the lips of some veterans of Gurney's California raceshop, although there were those crew members who followed Bobby when he left the California shop. So, too, there were in the end arguments and insults hurled between Bobby and Penske's crew chief, Derrick Walker.

Yet Bobby waxes enthusiastically, almost euphorically, over his three years with Roger Penske's

Two hundred laps after the green fell, Bobby accepted the jubilant congratulations of the crew. He'd won his first Indy. "It feels *so* neat (to win Indy), especially the first time. Nothing will ever be like that again."
BOBBY UNSER

Photo by Bill Stahl

team. "I did so *much* there," he says. "The three years there were worth 15 anyplace else. The most satisfying time of my entire career had to be the time at Penske's."

He says that was because of a "select group" of people. Among those Bobby singles out is Jim McGee, who ran Penske's team from 1974 through 1980. Bobby also tips his hat to Laurie Gerrish who was his chief mechanic over the three years he was with Penske, and to Jerry Breon, the team's chief fabricator—who became famous as the right rear tire changer on first Bobby's car and then on those of Rick Mears. There was a race at Michigan International Speedway in 1981: Breon was up all night, building a special exhaust system to Bobby's specifications in an effort to beat Penske teammates Mears and Mario Andretti. Says Breon, "Sure, Bobby is a hard man, and he pushes people to the maximum and maybe even beyond. But for a guy like that who goes out and produces in the race car, you do that type of thing." And Bobby did produce. During his three years as the Number One driver for the best team in Indycar racing, Bobby won 11 of 37 races and was on the pole (fastest qualifier) or front row 14 times—by all standards a phenomenal record.

Photo by Bob Tronolone

In 1975, after qualifying third, Bobby scored his second Indianapolis 500 win.

"This is the Super Modified again that belonged to the Foutz brothers. This is Louie, Jerry and myself. It's rare that Jerry would be home. That's why we'd be working on this car, you see. He had to be home on leave or just discharged or something."

BOBBY UNSER

"This is the 'Ugly Duckling' car in 1955 at Pike's Peak in the garage we were using. It was really my Super Modified that I won the Championship with—won a lot of races in Albuquerque—and we put a body on it and took it to Pike's Peak. That's Al on the right and the guy in the middle is a guy by the name of Bob Cropper. He was a mechanic."

(Bobby is on the left.)

BOBBY UNSER

Photo Courtesy of the Unser Family

In 1955 behind the wheel of the "Ugly Duckling," Bobby challenges Pike's Peak for the first time.

BOBBY UNSER

Photo Courtesy of the Unser Family

Bobby takes the checkered!

Photo Courtesy of the Unser Family

"This is 1956. Pike's Peak Hillclimb, 16 Milepost Turn. If you look at it, you can see how many people are up on this mountain. People will never believe how many people used to be there. You can just see, there's thousands of people."
BOBBY UNSER
Photo Courtesy of the Unser Family

Photo by Stewart's

"This is the Jaguar Pike's Peak car in 1956. I won the race that year. It was my first win (at Pike's Peak). In 1955 Louie drove it and the brake handle broke off. It was my car in the beginning, anyway, so I got it back in 1956. And I won with it—the brake handle didn't break. I won with that car in 1956 and 1958. In 1957, I finished third—we screwed up the rear suspension, made some modifications to it."
BOBBY UNSER
Photo Courtesy of the Unser Family

■ "Penske is one of the most feared men in the motor racing world because he's got a dedication like he does with all his businesses— nothing will stop him. I thought he was going to be terrible to work with, but he turned out to be a very fair man and I had so much fun with his team. If you had a bad series of engine problems or wrecks, that was when Penske would hold-out the toughest and work the hardest to get the problem solved. He doesn't sell his people down the river. To be involved with a guy like that had to be the pinnacle of my career.

"For a driver like myself who is so interested in all the many parts of racing, to have the power like I did with Penske, to have almost anything I wanted—well, that was fantastic. I'd never had anything like that in my entire life. Penske just opened up the whole book and gave it to me. He'd always answer the phone whether he was in a corporation meeting, with his family, on his airplane. He always wanted to know what

83

Photos by Carl Iwasaki

"These were shot for a magazine, 'Sports Illustrated' in 1956. Inside, it's the Jaguar engine, a bunch of trophies and (left to right) Al, Louie, Daddy, me, and Jerry.

"Outside, it's (left to right) Al, Louie, me, Daddy, and Jerry."

BOBBY UNSER

Photos Courtesy of the Unser Family

everyone was thinking. The later you called him, the better. If you called him at two in the morning with a bunch of ideas and things that you needed, he'd call you back first thing the next morning and it'd be check, check, check.

"That Penske is like a coyote. Once he smells blood, boy, you better watch out 'cause he'll start working so hard you can't believe it! He looks at success and money and winning races all under one roof. And if he sees something coming on, he'll check it three ways to make sure there wasn't a mistake made.

"Everybody predicted that Roger and I would be a bad team—I wasn't so sure myself. But it turned out the man was so straightforward and so clean whenever

85

"This would be me right here (#58) and that would be Al right there (#56). This would be a deal where he spun out, for what reason we don't know—it could be out of the picture—and I'm just trying to avoid him, and unable to do so. We obviously had a collision. But I don't even remember it.

"This is not a deal where Al and I are having a clash between us. I mean, I don't recall ever having any such animals, or any such circumstances or any such conditions."

BOBBY UNSER

Photo Courtesy of the Unser Family

"This particular year, 1957, we will have won every race of the season—one of the two of us. What had happened that year is that Al was racing—he was young, he was 18 or 19 years old—and some of the other drivers were collectively picking on him, and trying to use harsh means or devious ways to keep him from winning races: in other words, spin him out, block him, do whatever like that. And my dad and I went to Amarillo, Texas—we couldn't build a car real quick and we had to get one in a hurry—so we went to Amarillo, Texas, and bought that car (#58) and then fixed it up for me to run real quick. Then Al and I became a team against the others and from that day on, best I remember, we won every race there was. We'd switch off. I mean, one week it'd be his turn to win, the next week it would be my turn. And they stopped picking on Al."

BOBBY UNSER

Photos Courtesy of the Unser Family

86

Photo by Harry Kinney

Photo by Bob Tronolone

I dealt with him. I always knew where I stood. We also made a good team on the radio and in the pits. We thought alike. Sometimes I had to gamble on his decisions, but the more I got to know him, the more I knew it was worth the gamble.

"I was geared to go fast. I was geared to take the risk, to win the race against all comers. I was the torpedo for the team. Rick (Mears) was geared to step in and fill the breach if something happened to Bobby. Man, that was racing. That was what it's all about."

"That was my dad and me. This was 1959. This was the year that they found out that Al was too young (to drive Pike's Peak). See the number on the car? My number would have normally been like, a 58 or a 92. But 56 was Al's number.

"This was the first year that I owned my own race car. I got it from Jack Zink. Denny Moore built it, and I kept it at my dad's garage. And I put the thing together, now—we borrowed pieces from everybody you can imagine in order to get it together. And they caught Al, and I ran the car in the race and won with it. And I can remember the Grandview Motel because they sponsored the car. I was stone broke.

"That was the year I told you I won it. And (first wife) Barbara and I had less than a dollar between us. In other words, the Bobby Unser family had total monies, any way you went, of less than a dollar. Only had change—pocket change—totaling less than one dollar."

BOBBY UNSER

Photo Courtesy of the Unser Family

Bobby negotiates Riverside's Turn Seven in his Devin sports car during the 1958 running of the Riverside Grand Prix. "I always dreamed of road racing. My heroes were guys like Stirling Moss and Mike Hawthorn. These were the guys I wanted to beat. But coming from a poor family I just didn't have the opportunity to do much sports car racing."

BOBBY UNSER

Courtesy of the Unser Family

Bobby Junior earns an approving glance from Dad at Pike's Peak in 1957, the year in which Bobby interjected a third place finish between two wins.

Photo Courtesy of the Unser Family

Bobby at Pike's Peak in 1959.
(Note the improvised face mask.)
Photo Courtesy of the Unser Family

Photo by Carl H. Brattin

The highpoint of Bobby's time with Penske was undoubtedly his third and final victory at Indianapolis in 1981. He was dominant in that race, starting from the pole and leading powerfully almost all the way. It took nine months for Unser to be confirmed as the winner, however, after a dispute (see sidebar) over Bobby's method of rejoining the race following a pit stop made under a yellow flag. While Bobby, Penske and their lawyers argued their case in court, the rest of the season proved bitterly unlucky. In fact, although he led half of that year's races, he was not to win another Indycar event that year. So it is that his 1981 Indy 500 win stands as the last of Bobby's 35 Indycar victories.

"That race had a lot of meaning," says Bobby, "because I was ready way back in the winter. That

"This was a special Pike's Peak car. It's the car I got from Jack Zink of Tulsa—John Zink and Company—and I modified the car and changed it and put my own engines in it. This was in 1960."

BOBBY UNSER
Photo Courtesy of the Unser Family

"This was 1961 and I'm in the car I got from Jack Zink . The first year it had a Pontiac but now it's got a Chevrolet in it. It did make a difference. The Chevrolet was lighter and faster."

BOBBY UNSER
Photo Courtesy of the Unser Family

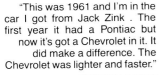

year's car was very touchy. There were a couple of tricks to making the thing handle, but all-in-all, it was good equipment and everything I did worked. It was just one of those deals where everything comes together. We didn't have any big fights over that race car. (Designer) Geoff Ferris and I got a little crossways over things, but it all went so well. I *knew* I had hold of things."

His first win at Indianapolis came in 1968 in an Offenhauser-powered Eagle owned by Bob Wilke. Chief mechanic on the car was Judd Phillips, who still builds Indycar engines.

"Now that was *fun*," says Bobby of his 1968 win in the 500. "Wilke was so good to me. He loved it when I won a race. He was an old-day Roger Penske. He ran a good, strong team in the '50s and '60s. I remember the winter before that race, I was sitting in Larry Truesdale's (Goodyear's racing chief at the time) office with Ed Alexander,

Bob Wilke and Judd Phillips. Nobody wanted to go with the turbo Offy that year—the Ford Motor Company was paying everybody who was any good a monthly salary to use their engines. And that was where—in Truesdale's office—we decided to turn down the monthly guarantee from Ford and take a chance on the turbo Offy.

Photo by Stanley L. Payne

"This is Louie (right) and me at the 1961 Pike's Peak hillclimb. He and I both won! He won the stock car division and I won the race car division. This was before Louie had MS.

"Louie was a better mechanic than he was a driver, though. He had fantastic mechanical abilities. Louie was one of those guys that really got into being able to learn mechanical things and figure out problems and innovate things that other people just couldn't do. So Louie would've always been a better mechanic than he would've been a race driver. He really has lots of abilities in mechanical stuff; a lot of good common sense that people didn't have."

BOBBY UNSER

Photo Courtesy of the Unser Family

89

"This is Al (#56) and me at Pueblo, Colorado in August, 1962. I'm driving the ECCA. That meant the Eloy Cotton Chemical Company, of Eloy, Arizona. Whoever drove this car got to Indianapolis. This car took about five or six drivers to Indianapolis. This car was so good that the drivers who drove it got such national attention, they got offers to run Indianapolis: myself, Al, Donnie Davis, (Danny) 'Termite' Jones, Roger McCluskey ... The car was fabulous and it was owned right here by a guy in Albuquerque by the name of Ron McGowen. He owned an engine rebuild shop in Albuquerque that's still here. He bought the car, and he and I maintained it, and he and I campaigned it. It was a big step in my career.

"I drove it when it was actually *the* ECCA car, but the guy was going broke. He was in the cotton chemical business Eloy—Cotton Chemical—and he couldn't make it at that, the business wasn't doing good. He wanted to sell the race car, and he wouldn't sell it just to anybody, he had such a personal attachment to the car. So Ron McGowen and I drove down there and talked to him, and he finally sold the car to Ron. The guy cried when we left with it. Then Ron and I fixed the car up, ran it out of my shop, and won lots of races with it, including this particular race."

BOBBY UNSER

Photo Courtesy of the Unser Family

Photo by Leroy Byers

"This would be a Midget race at Ascot in '63. And, I would be driving #4. Bud Trainor owned that, and he was another guy that was a big, big factor. He was the guy that got me in the ECCA car the first time. Then I immediately got attention. And he arranged and sponsored the thing so I could drive it's first race. And after that the guy who owned it hired me and then he went broke. Then Ron McGowen bought it. But that car just took me on a sequence of nice things.

"This (#99) is the car I ended up driving out there quite a bit. In fact, I won some races in that one. The #99 car was owned by Eddie Meyers, a famous old man."

BOBBY UNSER

Photo Courtesy of the Unser Family

"This was quite a wreck, probably around '63. It happened outside of Albuquerque, where the Tramway is now. And it was before they ever paved the road up there. It was a dirt road and I was testing. It was a brand-new rear engine car I'd just built. The first run ... There's the gas tank (leaning up against a tire)—it had flown off and gone some other place the injection stacks all bent ... over it was just a total, total, total wipe out. A brand new car! That was the very first run it ever made! I was in the hospital a while from that. But we built a new frame and built another car."

BOBBY UNSER

Photo Courtesy of the Unser Family

"OK, this would be the rear-engined car that I built. Remember that wadded up wreckage, all twisted around, of the Pike's Peak rear-engined car? This picture would be taken just a few hours before the crash, because it's on the way to do the test, right now. See? See this truck? This trailer, this truck, it's all out in the warehouse now, in storage there, where we stored them all."

BOBBY UNSER

Photo Courtesy of the Unser Family

Bobby at speed in 1963 participating in his first Indianapolis 500 in which he started 16th and was posted as finishing 33rd after an accident put him out of the running with two laps completed. On the third day he was the fifth fastest qualifier overall.

"This is the car that I took my (Indianapolis 500) driver's test in: the American Rubber and Plastics Special belonging to John Chalik. It was a terrible car, not capable of making the show. It wouldn't go fast enough . . . the guy was a weird old duck. It didn't take much money to run a car in those days, so the guy wasn't really spending a lot of money. But it did afford me my driver's test and I got through that fine. But the car wouldn't go fast enough to make the race. I got out of that and got into the Novi. There's my dad (at the rear of the car). We had big problems with that car. I obviously sat out a little too far, didn't I!"

BOBBY UNSER

Bobby tackles the dirt during the USAC 100 at Sacramento in October, 1962.

"Typical Bob Wilke," Bobby continues, "Whatever you want,' he said, 'it's yours.' Judd and I thought the Offy would be better, so everybody gambled on Bobby. We got the money from Truesdale, two engines, and ended up winning the race.

"We had a trick to going fast with that car and nobody could figure it out. Eventually, we had a *very* fast car. There was me and Lloyd Ruby and three turbine cars—all very fast.

"That was in the days when we carried 75 gallons of onboard fuel (compared to 40 gallons onboard capacity in today's Indycars). And when you hit the track you ran for a long time (before a pit stop for refueling). Those were the days when you got blisters on your hands!"

"This was at Pike's Peak in 1963, the year I ran Frank Arciero's Lotus 23 with a 2.7 Coventry Climax engine in it. And I set a new record with that.

"I was racing two divisions that day. I lost Pike's Peak very few times, I think I only lost it something like four times in my life, and that was one of my losses ... it in the sports car and lost it in the open wheeler that day.

"That was the first time a helicopter was used on Pike's Peak, going back and forth. And Al beat me in the race car division. I flew down and jumped into this (the Lotus) and won that and set a record."

BOBBY UNSER

In 1964, during Indy's maddening month of May, Bobby, ensconced in his Novi, chats with Andy Granatelli. Again, after starting 22nd on the grid, an accident put him out of contention after completing only one lap. He was credited with 32nd position.

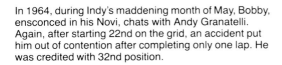

Bobby races Frank Arciero's Lotus 19 during the 1964 running of the Riverside Times Grand Prix.

92

Bobby (#28) and Bob Christie go at it during the USAC 100 at Phoenix in '64.

Thirty-year-old Bobby Unser.

At Sacramento in '65 Bobby (#88) has his eyes on two-wheeling brother Al (#40) who is followed by Jud Larson (#10) with AJ Foyt (#1) looming in the rear.

Bobby's Andy Granatelli-owned STP Novi is pushed out to vie for the 1965 Indianapolis 500. After starting the race from ninth position, he was sabotaged by a broken oil line and finished 19th.

Photo by Bob Tronolone

Bobby's "race face," circa 1966.

One of Bobby's treasures, a photograph of his daughter Cindy acting as Trophy Girl, presenting her father the winner's award after a Trophy Dash in Tucson, Arizona.

Photo Courtesy of the Unser Family

The results indicate that Bobby suffered no lack of vitamin C during Indy's 1966 month of May. He started the race in his Vita Fresh entry in 28th position and finished eighth.

Photo Courtesy of the Unser Family

95

Bobby digs in coming out of Sacramento's Turn Four in
1967.

Bobby (#91) and Mario Andretti duke it out down the
Phoenix straight in '66.

When Bobby won the 500 a second time seven years later with Dan Gurney's All-American Racers Team, it was the culmination of a period of dominance by driver and team. His win at Indianapolis in the rain-shortened 1975 Indy 500 was strategically brilliant and exactly the opposite of the front-running-but-car-breaking nature of Bobby's first two years (1971 and '72) with Gurney's factory Eagle team.

In 1971 and 1972, aboard Gurney's white Olsonite Eagle, Bobby established himself in history as one of the most aggressive, speed-hungry drivers ever seen in the sport. He was in the vanguard of some startling escalation in speeds as rapid advances in turbocharging and wing technology made for substantial increases in horsepower and downforce. Over 1100 BHP was used for qualifying in those days, and the rear tires were capable of breaking loose under acceleration at 190 MPH coming out of each of the four, 90-degree corners at Indianapolis. Amid these challenging circumstances, with lap speeds at Indianapolis increasing by 10 MPH and more over three successive years, Bobby and Gurney's AAR team set the pace. In 1972 Bobby spearheaded the assault on the 200 MPH barrier at the Ontario and Indianapolis Motor Speedways. And in the 21 Indycar races he started in 1971 and '72, he was on the pole 15 times! Victories were less numerous, however, and in neither year did Bobby win the national Championship. There was no doubt, however, that he was the speed demon of that halcyon time for Indycar racing.

97

#180 A,B

"This was my dad at Indy in 1967 in his 'Goodstone' jacket. I was Goodyear and Al was Firestone. They put 'Pop Unser' on the jacket: He was never called 'Pop Unser.' It was always 'Daddy.' Nobody ever called him 'Pop', except a couple of strange people."

BOBBY UNSER

Photo Courtesy of the Unser Family

Photo by Bob Tronolone

"That was in the pace car during the victory circle lap around Indianapolis (in 1968). And that would be (second wife) Norma, Bobby Junior and Cindy. They look so close alike—Bobby Junior and Robby, and Cindy and Jeri—look so close alike, I can't tell them apart at certain ages."

BOBBY UNSER

Photo Courtesy of the Unser Family

"This is me (#3), Roger McCluskey, and Art Pollard at Hanford, in March of 1968."

BOBBY UNSER

Photo Courtesy of the Unser Family

Photo by Bob Tronolone

In November, 1967, racing at Riverside, Bobby had
only dreams of the glories that awaited him a half year
away.

Brother Al and Sam Hanks greet Bobby as he enters
Indy's victory lane.

"This is Jud Phillips (left) and he, of course, is a very famous racing mechanic. And we're looking at the right front control arm which is coming apart. Boy, that thing's just shattering. That is the start of a *hell* of a wreck! This is the '67 Eagle, just by looking at the suspension."

BOBBY UNSER

Photo Courtesy of the Unser Family

"That would be the '67 Eagle at Phoenix in '68. We only had one '68 Eagle. So we ran this one. And this would have a Ford engine in it. Whereas the car I won Indianapolis with had an Offy in it."

BOBBY UNSER

Photo Courtesy of the Unser Family

Photo by Allen Photos

Bobby looks ahead to the back "straight" at Sacramento, September, 1968.

"This is 1968 in the Formula One BRM. I drove for the BRM factory ... I was heavy into road racing. The BRM wasn't a good car this year. It was a bad team for me to have driven for. But I'd done a contract and so I just finished the thing out, see. I did some testing for them in England and stuff like that. It just was a bad year to get involved with them and the cars were very uncompetitive. BRM used to go in and out of being mostly uncompetitive and occasionally competitive.

"That BRM bit you! It was a terrible race car. *I* wrecked one car, though. I broke my ankle the night before, playing basketball in Indianapolis during a race driver/press charity basketball game.

"I'm driving this car with a broken ankle and the doctor inside gave me real strong dope pills to take. I went in to get a novocaine shot, so that I wouldn't feel the pain in my ankle—it was my right one, that's the one you have to use on the throttle and the brake in these cars. And instead of giving me some novocaine, he gave me some really, really, worse goddamn pain tablets you can believe. I mean *terrible* dope. And I chunked down three or four of them. Didn't know what it was. He just said, 'Here, take these.' I wrecked that car so bad ... I mean, one of these just got totalled, I mean *bad* totalled. It's a wonder it didn't kill me.

"I didn't like Formula One as well. Formula One was very dangerous: they either had no fuel bladders or very, very light fuel bladders; very little safety stuff. In those days, Formula One was way behind Indycar racing, way behind. Their technologies weren't up with ours. Safety was, I venture to say, 10 years behind in those days. They used to just kill drivers like popped popcorn ... drivers used to just come and go over there just like nothing—like our Sprint cars used to do."

BOBBY UNSER

"This is Hanford in '68 and I'm getting a watch for being on the pole. That's J.C. Agajanian on my left."

BOBBY UNSER

101

"This is at Pike's Peak in '68. Nineteen-sixty-eight was the year that Louie built the engine for me. And that was really the real, real, real killer engine. It was a nitro burner . . . it was just a furious, furious race car. We ran 25 percent nitro in the engine and set a record that lasted for an ungodly amount of years. It was just . . . we were only gonna be there this year and we might not be back and if we are it would be many years and so we just really went after them. Louie wanted to build a real, real special engine. And he did it."

BOBBY UNSER

In 1973 and '74, progressive restrictions on turbo boost pressure and wing sizes worked against the advantages Bobby and Gurney had developed in '71 and '72. And at the end of '75, Bobby left Gurney's team, spending two years with Bob Fletcher's Cobre Tire outfit. Fletcher's team was a customer for Gurney's Eagles. Bobby leaped into the project in typical style, inspiring the independent team into doing engine, aerodynamic and chassis development. Against the odds, he won the 1976 California 500 with one of Fletcher's outdated but much modified Eagles. The following year, Fletcher was finally left behind by new cars and new engines. Bobby failed to win an Indycar race that year, 1977—the first time in 12 years he'd been a non-winner. In 1978, he returned to Gurney's factory team for one unhappy, unsuccessful year before signing to drive for Roger Penske, a prelude to three very successful, fulfilling years.

In sum, Bobby's career is the equal of the greatest drivers of the modern era: AJ Foyt, Mario Andretti, and of course, younger brother Al.

"What happened is that they had a rule that you could not run within either 24 or 48 hours—I think it was 24 hours—of a Formula One race, in any other event. It was something we didn't know about.

"See, what had happened was that we'd been over in Monza, Italy —Mario (Andretti) and I when I say, 'we'— to run the Formula One cars. And then we came back to run the Hoosier Hundred at Indianapolis at the Fair Grounds, and I did that, Mario and I both did. And when we went back to Italy, they would not allow us to start the race. The cars were there. We didn't get there 'til like 15 minutes before the race was supposed to start, anyway. It was that close of timing. So it was within the 24-hour period that Formula One had and they kicked us both out of the race because of that, see.

"So this is a telegram, obviously, from (second wife) Norma, 'Please give instruction what you want Mama— it should have said Mom—and I to do.' That's what it meant."

BOBBY UNSER

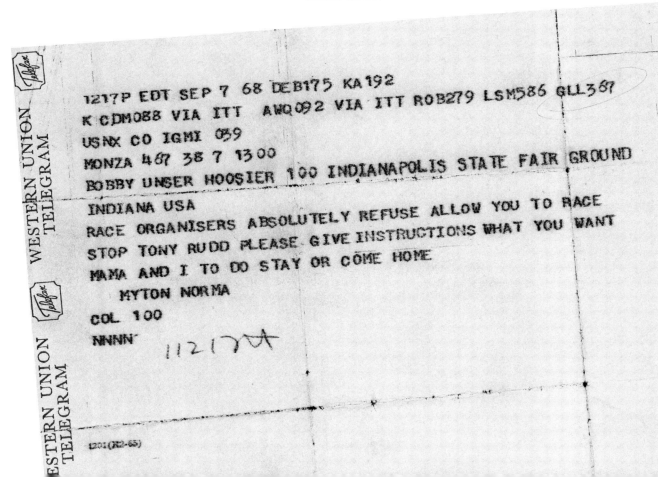

"Sixty-nine. The Hoosier 100."
BOBBY UNSER
Photo Courtesy of the Unser Family

Photo by Gene Crucean

"This would be at Milwaukee at a USAC late model stock car race—I can tell by the cooling duct. And what happened was that—there was Holman and Moody Ford—John Holman and Ralph Moody didn't get along too good and Ralph used to like to go run a race car of his own occasionally. So Ford Motor Company okayed the budget for running the car. I ran it for him like at the Indianapolis Fairgrounds, I ran it at Milwaukee, I ran it at a few places for them. And it was kind of like Ralph Moody's personal little deal, see. And we won the race that day at Milwaukee and we were running against the regular Ford racing team which would have been Holman and Moody. So it was a real big deal for us."

BOBBY UNSER

Photo Courtesy of the Unser Family

"This is (daughter) Jeri, about four months old."

BOBBY UNSER

"There I am, B. Unser, number 15 and doing a pit stop, during the Milwaukee 200 in '69 in Ralph Moody's personal car, you know, a '69 Ford. He was my personal friend, a smart man, good racer. He was a good race driver, besides, in those days, a damn good race driver.

"It was just a big deal for Ralph Moody to come up with his own car. And he'd select his own mechanics out of the shop then and he'd say, 'Come on. We're gonna go get Unser and we're gonna go race,' you know? Just occasionally we'd do that."

BOBBY UNSER

Photo Courtesy of the Unser Family

Photo by Gessert

Bobby dirt-tracking in 1969 at Sacramento.

Photo by Bob Tronolone

"This would be 1969 at Phoenix in the Bardahl Eagle, belonging to Bob Wilke," in which Bobby had eight top-five finishes, including one win.

BOBBY UNSER

Photo Courtesy of the Unser Family

Photo by Bob Tronolone

"This is me and Al at a Sprint car race, probably about 1969."

BOBBY UNSER

Photo Courtesy of the Unser Family

Photo by Lester Nehamkin

"This is 1969 and I'm presenting the (Indianapolis 500 winner's) ring to Mario (Andretti). He won the race that year, I won in 1968 so I'm presenting the ring to him. It was customary to do that." Bobby qualified and finished third that year.
BOBBY UNSER
Photo Courtesy of the Unser Family

Photo by Robert Young

"This is Andy Granatelli and myself at Trenton in 1970. This was during my last year with Wilke, in the Wagner car. And Andy, even though he was the president of STP, he also either ran or kind of controlled Wagner. And we're probably having an argument over money. I'm sure that's what it is."
BOBBY UNSER
Photo Courtesy of the Unser Family

Photo by Arnie deBrier

Bobby finds his mirrors filled with brother Al in his Ford-powered Colt at Phoenix in '71. In the 1971 version of the Olsonite Eagle-Offenhauser, Bobby won two races: the Milwaukee 200 and Trenton 300.

108

Five years older than Al, Bobby was born 15 months after twins Jerry Junior and Louie. By the time he was 18, he was winning races and Championships. At the age of 15, before he was old enough to hold a competition license, Bobby began gaining competitive experience by driving his father's cars in the annual Mexican road race. His father would start the race and then Bobby would slip behind the wheel and do all of the driving. "We had a system," Bobby tells the story, "where Daddy and I could change seats while still on the move."

The Mexican road races weren't without their share of adventure. During the race in 1952, his second year of competition, Bobby met the spectre of tragedy when a rambunctious driver hit the Unser entry as it was making a pass, lost control and careened over the

Photo by Bob Tronolone

roadside barriers into a rocky hillside. The Mexican driver was killed, and young Bobby was accused of murder in the Mexican press. Bobby received support from some unexpected sources. To this day, he remembers and is thankful for advice and consolation offered by a driver from Colorado, Loyd Axel. Following Bobby's return to Albuquerque, aerial photographs of the incident taken by a Mexican government plane, were made public, exonerating Bobby. And the young man received a letter of apology from the Mexican government for the disgrace that had been heaped on his shoulders.

It was also during the Mexican road race that Bobby met the face of love as personified by a beautiful young lady whom Bobby met when his car broke down almost in front of her family's home. There was no question in the lad's heart. It was hearts and flowers and "this is forever" love. When Bobby returned home, he found that the flame still burned as brightly as ever. He wrote his beloved informing her that he was on his way back to Mexico to marry her. He then informed his father of his decision. Apparently Daddy didn't say too much. He really didn't have to. In order to get a lower insurance rate, Bobby's car title was held in the name of his father's repair shop and under his father's control. Then, like now, Americans were not permitted to drive into Mexico in an untitled vehicle. Daddy revoked Bobby's car title and then informed all who might be so inclined that under absolutely no circumstances was Bobby to be loaned a car. And so for want of a title, the marriage never took place.

Bobby drove the Wagner/Lockheed Brake entry in the 1970 running of the Indianapolis 500, qualifying seventh and finishing 11th. He posted seven top-five finishes in '70, including a win in the Langhorn 150.   Photo by Bob Tronolone

Photo by Glenn Binegar

"That's Mario (right) and me, at the Hoosier 100 in 1970. This (center) was a preacher, Hershell West, a real neat guy. He used to go to all the races with Mario and me. You see, Mario and I used to be real close friends. We used to travel together an awful lot. We used to go to Sprint car races, Dirt car races, all the races together. We were very close friends. Wished I could remember that guy's name.

"This guy, Glen Binegar the photographer, was one of the best friends I ever had. He died. He had a heart attack. A lot of our pictures, a lot of them nice pictures, have Binegar's name on them."

BOBBY UNSER

Photo Courtesy of the Unser Family

Bobby gets ready to qualify his Olsonite Eagle for the 1972 Indy 500 as chief mechanic Wayne Leary checks out the cockpit. "Wayne was one of the best chiefs ever."

BOBBY UNSER

110

"This is President Nixon's daughter, Tricia, at Ontario at the California 500 in 1972. We politicked for Nixon. This is her husband (far left) and Ozzie Olson (second from left, partially hidden, Bobby's car owner). I presented a helmet to President Nixon via her. He was supposed to come to the races but didn't."

BOBBY UNSER

Photo Courtesy of the Unser Family

Photo by Richard George

Bobby in race-day Indy trim in 1972. After qualifying on the pole with a speed of 195.940 MPH, a broken distributor rotor knocked him out of the running.

Photo by Bob Tronolone

"This is John Miller. He's like almost genius in status. He has no education and the man has just performed miracles. *He's* the guy that we can attribute most of our records to in 1972 when we sat on the pole every race. I found him when we went to Hawaii this (1987) summer. Very much of a loner, just a complete loner person. And just so smart you can't believe it."

BOBBY UNSER

Photo Courtesy of the Unser Family

In 1972, Bobby broke the 200 MPH barrier with a qualifying speed of 201.374 at Ontario Motor Speedway. A broken engine put him out of the running, however, after completing only 73 laps. Following his qualifying run for the Cal 500, Bobby poses with his crew, (from left) crew chief Wayne Leary, team owner Dan Gurney, engine builder John Miller, and the other team mechanics.

By the time he was 20 years old, Bobby was already a very experienced driver with a wealth of life's experiences already to his credit. Modified stock car Champion of New Mexico in 1950 and '51, he had his eyes set firmly on Pike's Peak where his Uncle Louis held so many records. "That was the thing that motivated me in those days," recalls Bobby. "Back then I didn't really even think about the Indianapolis 500. I wanted to beat my Uncle Louis at Pike's Peak."

In 1955, Jerry Unser took his three oldest sons to Pike's Peak, and the following year, Bobby began his successful assault on his uncle's record of victories at the Peak. Pike's Peak winner in '56, he proceeded to sweep the hill-climb six years in a row, from 1958 through 1963.

As his reputation grew, Bobby began to pursue a wider range of racing. He established himself as an outstanding Sprint car driver, and in order to run more races and be able to commute regularly to California, he learned how to fly, buying a succession of small airplanes. "I had enough of driving 18 hours to the west coast. That kind of thing began to wear me down, so I decided I had to learn to fly. And that opened up a whole new world to me. The only way a guy could live in a place like Albuquerque and go after a career in racing was to be able to fly."

"This would have been Pocono, Pennsylvania. Al (right) is running for Vel's Parnelli Jones, and that's Mark Donohue (center). And this is in the year 1973. I didn't win it. That race eluded me for a long time."
BOBBY UNSER
Photo Courtesy of the Unser Family

In 1963, Bobby was ready to follow his late brother Jerry's footsteps to Indianapolis. By that time, he was almost 30 and as impassioned and aggressive a driver as ever. He drove for a variety of teams and had his share of experience with new ideas, four-wheel drive, super-charging and turbocharging. He experienced the extremely powerful, ear-piercing Novi engine driving for Andy Granatelli's STP team for three years. He ultimately established himself with Bob Wilke's team for a four- year period, 1966-70, and won the '68 Indianapolis 500, beating Mario Andretti to that year's national Championship by 11 points—4,326 to 4,315.

Bobby's uncompromising style of racing earned him the family nickname of "Rommel," in memory of the great German Field Marshal who made his reputation in the deserts of north Africa during World War II. His demanding personality was also a factor in the demise of his first marriage. First wife Barbara Schumacher gave birth to two children, a son, Bobby Junior and a daughter, Cindy. Bobby was divorced from Barbara after 12 years, however, and shortly thereafter he married Norma Davis who bore him another son, Robby,

and a daughter, Jeri. Norma was not much interested in racing. Thus, after four years, this marriage also ended in divorce. Since 1975, Bobby has been married to Marsha Allison Sale, a petite, sharp-humored, dark-haired woman from Mesa, Arizona. Marsha was an avid supporter of her husband's racing career and doubles, these days, as Bobby's personal secretary and organizer.

Since he retired from racing Indycars, Bobby has assumed a slightly more relaxed attitude toward life. He continues to spend at least half of any year on the road, making personal appearances, plugging products and working first for NBC and now ABC Sports. He plays as hard as ever on his snowmobiles and other toys, and prefers any project with which he's involved to be done in a thorough, complete manner. But, in retirement, Bobby is a more fulfilled person. He is capable of laying back and enjoying small moments and aspects to life rather than pushing every opening for the maximum opportunity. It is inaccurate to use the word, "mellow," to describe Bobby Unser's retirement, but there is now an element of that in Bobby's world.

114

"That's Marsha and Mom and me at Michigan in 1973."
BOBBY UNSER

Photo Courtesy of the Unser Family

Needless to say, it took some time for this "mellowing" to take effect. The year after Bobby quit driving for Penske, he ran young Mexican driver Josele Garza's Indycars out of his raceshop, located in front of his Albuquerque home on Route 66. Inevitably, young driver and dyed-in-the-wool racer frequently argued and butted heads. At Indianapolis that year (1982), Bobby even climbed aboard one of Garza's cars for a few laps in an effort to squeeze more speed from the machine. At the end of the year, Bobby and Garza dissolved their relationship with Bobby declaring he should never be involved with the running of another man's race car, "unless he's an Unser." Today, Bobby expounds, "Josele was a nice, nice person. His whole family, they were all nice people, but he just didn't understand about *racing*, about being fast, about being the best."

"This would be on Harold Holl-nagel's boat. I do consulting work for a company called Mechanical Industries in Milwaukee, Harold Hollnagel's. He's been one of my longest, best friends. It's a fishing trip—we're back for a race—and we're doing PR work for some of his customers."

BOBBY UNSER

Photo Courtesy of the Unser Family

Marsha, in Milwaukee's Victory Circle, experiencing her first win with Bobby, June, 1973. "Gee, I forgot her hair was like that!"

BOBBY UNSER

Photo Courtesy of the Unser Family

"This is a picture of Robby and Jeri sent to me in the hospital in 1973 the time I had a very, very bad wreck at PIR. The car just broke into little pieces, and I came very close to not making it that time.

"I've only had a couple (of accidents) that were really bad, one in Phoenix—I've had more than one bad wreck—but as far as getting hurt, that particular time and one time in a go kart I got hurt really bad. Yeah, with no helmet on. Screwing around too, not in a race, just screwing around.

"That should have never happened, but it did and that laid me up for a year. I wore a patch over my eye for six months. Broke my skull open and the spinal fluid was running out my ears. That was in 1959. My brother had just died in Indianapolis and just a little bit later, I was in the hospital, almost dead myself."

BOBBY UNSER

Photo Courtesy of the Unser Family

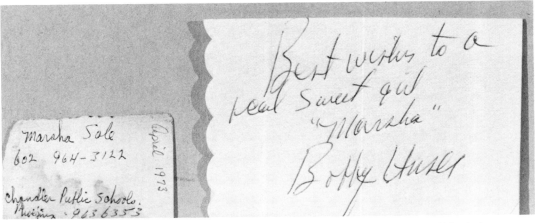

Best wishes to a real sweet girl "Marsha"
Bobby Unser

Marsha Sale
602 964-3122

Chandler Public Schools
Arizona · 963 6353

April 1973

A moment immortalized in Bobby and Marsha's scrapbook: Arizona art teacher Marsha Sale wanted to get an autograph from Bobby Unser for one of her students. Not only did her student receive the treasured autograph, Marsha also was presented with the famous signature. But in return, a trade being a trade, Bobby received Marsha's phone number and squirreled it away in his wallet. Three years later, Miss Sale became Mrs. Unser.

Photo by Bob Tronolone

Testing an experimental rear wing at Ontario in March of '74, Bobby was nothing if not cooperative when it came to expanding the limits of technology through trying and testing.

"On my way to Ontario's victory circle in '74."
BOBBY UNSER

Courtesy of the Unser Family

Tony Hulman and Bobby pose in Ontario's victory circle after Bobby's first Cal 500 win.

Photo by Bob Tronolone

■ "I think every designer I've ever run into has a reasonable amount of jealousy in him. You know: If the guy didn't think of the idea that made the race car go fast, then it wasn't a good idea. Sometimes I think designers can be far too touchy about who comes up with the ideas. I've watched designers deliberately take something they know is wrong and work around the problem because I wanted to solve the problem in another way.

"I'm not a trained engineer, so I have to do my development work a little bit different than they might. But it's really just a process of elimination—try a high camber curve, a low camber curve. See what works. I would have 50 percent failures in my development work but you've got to expect that. Each failure is a lesson learned. It gives you a different direction. It really isn't any different than the original American way of doing things: Keep trying, always keep trying. If you work hard enough, you'll find it."

117

In 1980 Bobby started 11 Indycar events. He finished in the top three eight times, including four wins.

At the wheel of his Norton Spirit PC9 Cosworth, Bobby's four 1980 wins included his fourth Cal 500 victory. He finished second in the national standings, and that year went over the $2 million mark in Indycar earnings.

At age 45, Bobby had rediscovered the joys of winning.

After being absent from the winner's circle for two years, Bobby returned with a vengence in 1979, scoring six wins, including one at Watkins Glen.

FOSTER

Unser v

The California 50C

Ontario Motor Speedway knew a good advertising
gimmick when they saw one.

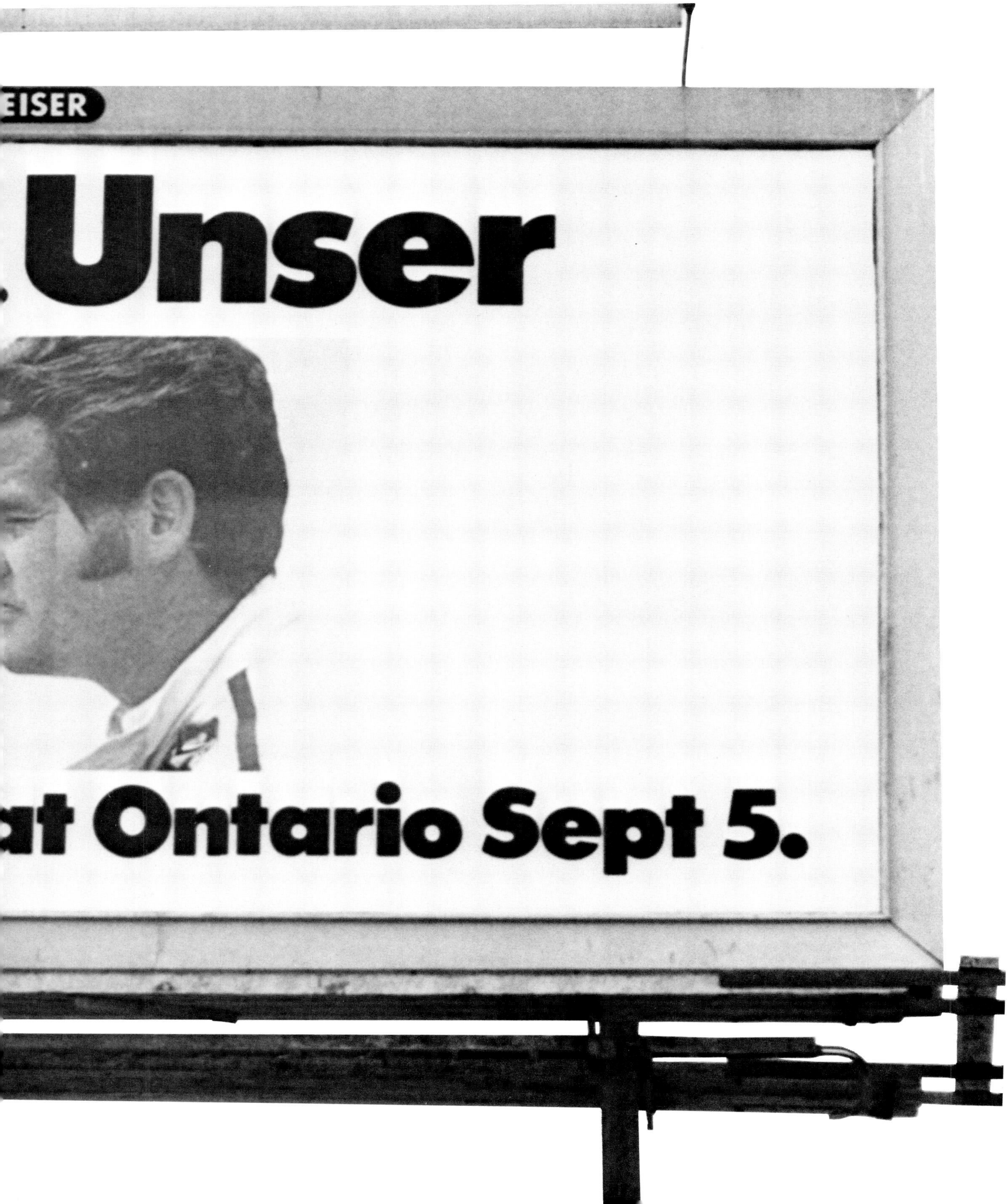
EISER
Unser
at Ontario Sept 5.

"This is the famous Teddy Yip, Marsha and me in Hong Kong in 1977. We've been exceptionally close friends for many years. And what he does, he puts on a race in Macau, the Macau Grand Prix. And for quite a few years, Marsha and I went over there. I would be the celebrity at hand with Teddy Yip for the Macau Grand Prix. And Hong Kong, you see, is the jumping off place for Macau.

"Teddy and I have been literally all over the world together. He's come to the ranch, he's snow-mobiled with us, he's been to Albuquerque many times, we've done a lot of business, industrial deals together. He's the closest of friends.

"He's owned race cars, incidentally. He used to own Formula One cars, Indycars—he was the owner of my Indycar one year."

BOBBY UNSER

Photo Courtesy of the Unser Family

"This was one of (Marsha's and my) deer, Sassy. She was the little girl deer that we raised."

BOBBY UNSER

Photo Courtesy of the Unser Family

October, 1979. "These are fawns that Marsha—mainly Marsha, I should say—raised. They were orphans and we did this for the State Game and Fish (Department) of New Mexico. I guess we were one of the very few people in the state that knew how to raise deer in captivity. They have a very bad habit of just dying on you in captivity. They don't do well. We owned, at that particular time, three of our own—maybe four, it depends on whether one of them had had a pup or not. We had raised, of our own up to this time, three of them. We kept two of them, which we had for eight years. These particular ones that you're looking—at this is in our back yard, and we put this tem-porary fence across in order to kind of contain them a little bit, probably keep them out of Mar-sha's flowers, I guess—and we used to have to feed them every four hours, 24 hours every day, seven days a week. See where they stick their tails up in the air when they eat—straight as a board."

BOBBY UNSER

Photo Courtesy of the Unser Family

Photo by Jutta Fausel

Photo by Jutta Fausel

Photo by Jutta Fausel

"We (Marsha and Bobby) were at the SEMA show in Las Vegas in 1976 and about mid-way through the day, I just decided to get married ... I shouldn't say mid-way, probably afternoon, mid-afternoon. And the guy who was the in-house attorney at the Las Vegas Hilton, Frank Shattuck, was a very close friend of mine—still is—and I just got ahold of Frank and I said, 'Can you arrange for me to get married?'

"And he said, 'When?'

"And I said, 'Just as soon as possible. An hour, two hours, something like that.' And that's how it happened. I got Marsha and put her into a cab—both of us—and we started downtown. And she said, 'Where are we going?'

"And I said, 'We're going down to get a marriage license. We're gonna get married today.' And that's what hap-pened. That was a neat time."

BOBBY UNSER

Photo Courtesy of the Unser Family

"This photo is in November of '79, me and Cosworth.

BOBBY UNSER

Photo Courtesy of the Unser Family

122

"This is Josele Garza (right) and me at Riverside in 1982. The problem here was that Josele was just a young kid, he was not even 21 years of age, yet. Nice boy—his whole family, all of his friends, everybody was *really* nice. We had a nice race team. But he just wasn't a racing driver yet. And I was used to winning races and going too fast. I just was not able to accept trying to have the car in good shape and the car capable of going fast, and he just couldn't go fast in it. We tried different cars, we tried everything and it just was no good. It was the most miserable year, racing-wise, that I've ever had in my life. I just absolutely hated that year. There was no amount of money that was worth not winning races, to me.

"Above all, Josele was a nice person. He was learning and he was not capable then. I didn't realize, for example, how important race drivers were. I was a race driver all of my life. I don't think, in all of my years of motor racing, I ever figured out why people paid a racing driver so much money, until Josele came along. When I did that deal with Josele, all of a sudden it dawned on me what race drivers were really worth. Because it made no difference what we did. It was virtually an impossibility to win a race.

"The whole fault of that whole thing was *me* having the attitude that I could make a race car go fast no matter what.

BOBBY UNSER

Photo Courtesy of the Unser Family

Bobby's good friend, Harold Hollnagel, president of Mechanical Industries of Milwaukee, Wisconsin, shared a few moments with Bobby before the running of the '81 Indy 500. Bobby has served since the early 1970s as automotive adviser for Mechanical Industries.

Photo Courtesy of Mechanical Industries

Pictured at Road America, in 1981 Bobby put his Norton Spirit on the pole for the Indianapolis 500 with a qualifying speed of 200.546 MPH.

The following winter, Bobby decided he wanted to race again and talked to Indycar team owner Pat Patrick about the 1983 racing season. In December of '82, he tested one of Patrick's cars at Phoenix International Raceway. He wasn't happy or comfortable with the old surroundings and, after a few days of thought, Bobby decided to write a letter of resignation to Patrick. In that uncharacteristically reticent way, Bobby Unser made his final decision to retire from racing Indycars.

Three seasons later Bobby, having agreed to do some developmental work for Audi on the 4WD turbocharged Audi Quattro, returned to competition. At the Talladega, Alabama superspeedway, he lapped a production-based Audi at 206.8 MPH. Then, after having been away from the hillclimb for 12 years, Bobby took an Audi Quattro to Pike's Peak. There, he reclaimed the hill record, winning the event overall a resounding, record-setting tenth time.

Bobby qualified his Olsonite Eagle seventh on the grid for the 1974 Indianapolis 500. He finished second.

"This was in 1974, Pike's Peak and this car was built by Harry Hyde of NASCAR fame. And it was the K & K Insurance Company race car. It was run by K & K with all their rig and their racing team, but it was really a Dodge factory effort.

"They built a car specifically for Pike's Peak. It was a kit car—of course they were Grand National kit cars—but this one was done special for Pike's Peak. You know, the tubing in it was all thin wall tubing, not like the Grand National which would be like the .125-thou' wall. This one would be like an .080-thou' wall. I mean, we tried stuff on that car that was just really . . . its still working for Harry Hyde now. He is a very smart man."

BOBBY UNSER

Photo Courtesy of the Unser Family

124

"This is Marsha (left), Mom (center) and me at a chili deal out in California in 1975. We were doing pictures for Ortega, which is a Heubline company."

BOBBY UNSER

Photo Courtesy of the Unser Family

"This is 1975 and that's Parnelli Jones (receiving a tortilla). That's Marsha (left), me and Parnelli. What we're doing is, we used to have yearly chili cookouts. And we did it in the Poconos every year. This was down at Greenwall Lodge, where the people who own that place—Ron and Jeanette Sarajian—are very close friends of ours. So we're using their rec room and we cook the chili right in their kitchen.

"Everybody used to come to that. God! I mean, they'd look forward to that more than anything you could believe."

BOBBY UNSER

Photo Courtesy of the Unser Family

Bobby gave new meaning to the phrase, "Up close and personal," coined by ABC, the network with which he's currently affiliated, when he filled AJ Foyt's mirrors to overflowing during the 1976 running of the Daytona IROC event.

■ More than four months passed between the time that Bobby entered victory lane at Indianapolis on May 24, 1981, and the day in October that an appeal board declared him as the official winner of the 65th Indianapolis 500.

The evening of the race, USAC officials studied television videotapes of the 500 and when the official results were published at 8 o'clock the following morning, Bobby was listed in second place behind Mario Andretti. Penalized one lap for his method of rejoining the race after a pit stop, Bobby spent much of the summer with team owner Roger Penske's lawyers, fighting the decision before a three-man appeal board.

Bobby was the dominant man at Indianapolis that year. He qualified on the pole 125 and led most of the race, battling hard with Patrick Racing teammates Mario Andretti and Gordon Johncock. Three-quarters of the way through the race under a yellow caution flag, Bobby came into the pits in company with Andretti. Bobby's stop was a few seconds

At Pike's Peak in 1983, Unser cousins and brothers—drivers and coaches—pose: (left to right) Bobby Junior, Bobby, Al, and Al Junior.

Photo by David Hutson

"That's Bobby Junior's daughter, Jesse. She's a little darling. I don't think (being a grandfather) changes me at all. I don't see any reason for it, really. They call you 'grampa' and they tease you. But I think it's kinda neat because she's neat, see?
BOBBY UNSER

"Third generation . . . "
MARSHA UNSER

"They get along great!"
BOBBY UNSER, JR.

"She's really a nice little girl. She does have the devil in her, I'll guarantee that!"
BOBBY UNSER

Photo Courtesy of the Unser Family

quicker than Mario's so that he led the sprint out of pit lane. As he accelerated along the apron inside the first turn, Bobby came upon a pack of cars, running slowly in the groove behind the pace car. Before pulling into line Bobby passed four of the cars running behind him, Andretti also passed a couple of cars before pulling into line. When the race was restarted Bobby continued to set the pace, pulling away to win easily from Andretti, who lost time with a soft tire and weakening engine. Johncock kept the pressure on Bobby until seven laps from the end when his engine blew, thus Bobby came home a convincing winner, eight seconds ahead of Andretti.

"This was on July 10, 1986, qualifying day at Pike's Peak with the Audi Quattro. I set a new record that day, four minutes, 53.67 seconds."
BOBBY UNSER
Photo Courtesy of the Unser Family

"This was at Pike's Peak and that's my daughter, Jeri. And this is after we won (in the Audi, July 12, 1986). Jeri just loves racing. I don't think she's the one who should have been a race driver, but she'd rather go to a race than anything else. I think she likes racing—going to the races—more than anybody in any of our families."
BOBBY UNSER
Photo Courtesy of the Unser Family

"This is Cindy, my oldest daughter (on the left), and Bobby Junior (on the right), and Marsha and myself at the Pikes Peak awards banquet on July 12, 1986."
BOBBY UNSER
Photo Courtesy of the Unser Family

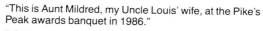

"This is Aunt Mildred, my Uncle Louis' wife, at the Pike's Peak awards banquet in 1986."
BOBBY UNSER
Photo Courtesy of the Unser Family

Following Bobby's victory in the Phoenix 150, Bobby, Marsha and team owner Bob Fletcher pose for photographers.

Bobby (#6) and Al at Phoenix in October, 1977. At the '77 running of Indy, Bobby qualified a most respectable second but was relegated to the 18th finishing position when an oil leak put him out of the race.

At Indy in '76, Bobby qualified 12th and finished 10th. However, it was in this same car, after qualifying 10th, that he won his second Cal 500.

"This is in between our shots at the Speedway in '87. What we're doing is looking at the monitor waiting to go on. What we didn't realize that's kinda funny about this—Lampley was the worst—but he's sitting there making faces, watching himself in the monitor. He's making faces, doing all kinds of funny things and it's going all over the world. Not in the homes, but like on cable television, like satellite Telestar One—I mean it goes all over. Everybody at the Speedway, in the suites and everything, was watching us that day, thank God I was straight, but Lampley was acting up. God, they teased him about that!"
BOBBY UNSER
Photo Courtesy of the Unser Family

Bobby and Al Junior share opinions during the '87 season.

If a driver is deemed to have passed illegally under the yellow flag, he is usually penalized during the running of the race, either by a one-lap penalty or a timed, black flag penalty wherein the guilty party is compelled to pull in and stop at his pit while the race carries on under the green flag. This method of penalizing provides the driver with an opportunity to make up the time lost to the penalty over the remaining race distance. USAC's immediate post-race ruling robbed Bobby of this opportunity. Also, the posting or reversing of decisions by studying videos after a race or sporting event is usually considered a bad practice. And too, there was much discussion about the "blend-in" rule: Three-time Indy-winner Johnny Rutherford told the hearings that no firm resolution to the "blend-in" rule was ever announced during any drivers' meetings.

129

Making his way to Ontario's victory circle, a third Cal 500 win was included in Bobby's '79 tally of six victories.

Photo by Bob Tronolone

"This would be the ARCO Graphite car, 1978. Gurney built two of them that year. This was the first one that he built. Extremely unsuccessful.

"This was taken at Ontario. He made the front end look like an Eagle. See how the eyes are? It was theoretically a modern-day Eagle. That was the one that was owned by Teddy Yip. He took the same tub, did away with all the bodywork. It looks like he built two cars, it was really one car with a modification done."

BOBBY UNSER

Photo Courtesy of the Unser Family

Bobby and Al confer on Michigan's pit wall.

Photo by Marc Sproule

"This would be Marsha and me, 1981, Indianapolis, my third Indy win!" ... Eventually. A few more instances of bureaucratic thinking and the Unsers might almost have been indicating how many times Bobby won the one event.

BOBBY UNSER

In the end, USAC's appeal board decided to rescind the one-lap penalty levied against Bobby. A 23-page summation was issued by the appeal board and Bobby was fined $40,000. Also, the cost of the hearings was assigned by the three-man appeal panel to Penske Cars Ltd. Nevertheless, after a long summer of debate, Bobby was reinstated as the winner of the 1981 Indianapolis 500. It was his third win at Indianapolis and the 35th and last win of his long career in Indycars.

Bobby ready to go to work.

Promoting the sport of snowmobiling and Ski-Doo snowmobiles, the Unsers are main attractions at the Eagle River, Wisconsin World Snowmobile Championship, snowmobile racing's Indianapolis 500. Enjoying a laugh as the celebrity parade begins at the 1988 World Championship are (left to right) Russell M. Davis, national sales manager for Bombardier Corporation; Al Junior; Al; Wayne Kester, Bombardier Corporation's communications manager; and Bobby. (Bombardier Corporation is the U.S. subsidiary of Bombardier, Inc., the maker of Ski-Doo snowmobiles.)

Highlights of Bobby's career in trophies and mementos: three Indianapolis 500 victories and four Cal 500 wins.

Bobby and Marsha's Albuquerque living room.

133

Bobby's win at the Peak in 1986 stood him forever ahead of his old rival, Uncle Louis. First of all, he had broken the tie of nine overall victories apiece, shared by him and his uncle. Together with his two stock car class victories (1969 and 1974) and single sports car class win (1963), his win with the Audi brought his total number of Pike's Peak victor's trophies to an incredible 13. On all but one of those occasions, Bobby set a new record.

At the awards dinner that evening, Bobby wore an emotional glow. "It's really good to come back to your roots," he said. "To be able to come back with such a tremendously competitive team and to be able to go after the record without any restrictions has been as important to me as anything that has happened in my whole career, including my three wins at Indianapolis."

Earlier in the day, back at the base of the mountain after his record-setting climb, Bobby described the run: "This was as good a run as I've ever had here," he said. "There were no mistakes, no missed shifts. I'm really happy with the way it went. Like I've been saying all week, the car is very sensitive to adjustments, and we made two very small changes in setup this morning, both of which worked well.

"I think that if we had had just a little bit of rain at the top like we had at the bottom of the hill last night, it would have been possible to break 11 minutes. As it was, the car was very loose from the 16 mile mark all the way to the top. There was just nothing on the road surface for the tires to get hold of.

"Through the last turn and over the finish line I got very wide and loose, and there were people jumping out of my way. But all the way up there was just a tremendous crowd. There were people cheering everywhere. I've never seen so many people cheering. It was really touching, really moving. I tried not to let it affect me, but inside I could feel it."

Now apparently retired from driving Indycars for good, Bobby continues to visit many Indycar races in his capacity as a commentator for ABC Sports. His informed and opinionated comments are lively, cogent and much appreciated by racing fans. There is no doubt that the theater of American motor racing, without Bobby Unser, would have been, and would continue to be, a much duller place.

Having walked away from Indy-car driving, Bobby develops his skill in Indycar broadcasting as he interviews Al at Phoenix in 1983 for NBC-TV.

Photo Courtesy of the Unser Family

Photo by Bob Tronolone

At 200 mph this is the car Bobby Unser believes in.

Ask three-time Indy winner Bobby Unser what it takes to drive at speeds over 200 mph and you're unlikely to hear him talk about courage. The word he mentions most often is confidence.

Which is why it is no small coincidence that the car he recently set a new all-wheel drive speed record in was a specially modified, production-based Audi Quattro.

It gave Bobby Unser something just as important as tremendous power.

The confidence to use it. By way of the unique Quattro system of permanently engaged all-wheel drive.

Even at speeds in excess of 200 mph, this Audi handles with a composure that, according to Bobby Unser, approaches nonchalance.

"It is rock steady and razor sharp," says Unser. "At speeds like this, a car without four-wheel drive will normally break loose in the turns. With the Quattro I'm able to keep the power applied and come out of the turns faster. With control."

While Unser's Quattro was specially modified, it utilized the same basic full-time, all-wheel drive technology found on all our Quattros.

Now, if Bobby Unser believes in this Audi innovation at over 200 mph, just imagine how it handles at 55.

You see, when it comes to delivering power, mobility, grip and control, four driven wheels can be superior to two. Or as Unser puts it, "drive a Quattro for a while and you'll never want to go back to two-wheel drive again."

Quattro technology is the kind of fresh creative thinking that has placed Audi at the forefront of engineering originality.

It's far from conventional four-wheel drive simply rehashed.

It's four-wheel drive totally refined, rethought and practically reinvented.

Which is precisely what the Audi philosophy of challenging the old and discovering the new is all about.

The Quattro system isn't better because it's different.

It's different because it's better.

It overcomes the inherent drawbacks and limitations of typical four-wheel drive vehicles.

It isn't noisy, ungainly or mechanically harsh.

And it doesn't look like it's riding on stilts.

As a matter of fact, it's everything four-wheel drive was never supposed to be.

Comfortable, graceful and an unadulterated joy to drive.

Here in America, we've gone from offering one Quattro model seven years ago to the availability of five today: the 5000CS Turbo Quattro, 5000CS Turbo Quattro Wagon, the 5000S Quattro and the new 80 and 90 Quattros.

To put it all into perspective, in 1980 the automotive pundits questioned why we were putting full-time all-wheel drive in our high performance cars.

Today, the very same pundits are questioning why it has taken the competition so long to put it in theirs.

Audi

Al and Karen in the 1 [...]
apolis 500 victory cir[...]

Photo by Bill Stahl

Seeing California the fast way…taking a Laguna Seca corner all out!

Al Unser

Al makes a pitstop at the Meadowlands, New Jersey on the way to his 1985 National Championship.

aby Al was the kid brother. Jerry and Mary Unser's three older sons played together, went to school together, competed in sports together, fought and raised hell together. They also started racing cars about the same time, all three of them deeply into the sport by the time Al was old enough to begin to think seriously about driving and racing.

That somewhat isolated position in the family gave Al a slightly different perspective on life than his older brothers. Based on what he has achieved in racing and on the way in which Al has gone about doing those things, it might be fairly said that his kid brother role probably helped him accumulate, synthesize and dispense more racing wisdom than any other Unser. For one thing, he has achieved a great deal over a long and continuing period of time. For another, there are the hallmarks of Al's driving style—ultra-smooth, canny, keen-minded. He's capable of making the best of a situation, of bringing the car home in one piece. He is an absolutely relentless driver. And of course, he has raised a successful race-driving son with whom he carved out a unique chapter in automobile racing history when the duo battled for the national Championship down to the last lap of the last race in 1985.

Consider that Al has not only won four Indianapolis 500s (equalling AJ Foyt's record), but

that he is also tied with Ralph DePalma (a great driver from the early 1900s through the 1930s) for first place in the laps led category at Indianapolis. Furthermore, at the end of the 1987 racing season, he had won more money not only at Indianapolis, but also in the history of Indycar racing. Consider also that Al is the only man to have won all three Indycar 500 mile races in a single year (1978) and that he has placed among the top three in a grand total of 19 500-mile races. At Indianapolis alone, he finished five of the six 500s run between 1982 and 1987 in the top five and ran 2,860 of a possible 3,000 miles! He also shares the record (again with Foyt) for the most wins (10) in a single Indycar season (1970) and earned a reputation at that time as one of the finest practitioners ever seen of the art of dirt track racing. Beyond that, he's won Formula 5000 and Can-Am road races, taken the Indycar national title three times over a 15 year period and established himself, by winning the 1985 CART title and 1987 Indianapolis 500, as the sport's greatest, most appreciated "backup driver."

In the middle of all this, the key word perhaps is versatility. Al has demonstrated that facility over his entire career and particularly in 1970, the last year in which dirt track races were included in the national Championship. Al won all five dirt races that year and also won on a road course (Indianapolis Raceway Park, one of three road races that year), a superspeedway (Indianapolis), and on paved, one mile or 1.5 mile ovals (Phoenix, Milwaukee and Trenton).

■ *"Hardly in the history of racing have you ever had two brothers like Bobby and me—really it was all four of us. Jerry was a very competitive driver and Louie was, too. But to have two brothers do what Bobby and I have done and then all of a sudden our sons come along and do it, it makes you wonder. Is it because they're an Unser or Andretti or whatever?*

"I don't know. I have no idea. I wish I could answer that and say it's because of this or that. I think basically it's total desire that makes a race car driver. It's what a man wants to do from within himself. That's where it comes from."

139

Victory!

"That was one of the donkeys we used to have. My brothers used to tie me on mine because I was so little, and I always wanted to go with them and they didn't want me to go because they always had to take care of me. They used to tie me on and when I would fall off, this thing would drag me through cactus and everything, which happened many times. And they thought it was funny!"

AL UNSER

Photo Courtesy of the Unser Family

1947-48

1948-49

"This had to be in Washington Junior High. I played fullback, halfback. I played on into high school until I quit high school. Yeah, I loved football—it was neat—but not more than cars, not hardly."

AL UNSER

Photo Courtesy of the Unser Family

"That's (during the Mexican Road Race) Louie and Bobby, some Mexican, Daddy and Mom and me (taking a photograph). Mom drove the chase car and I rode with her. I was being … how do you put it … I was set down. I couldn't do anything down there. I did something wrong in school. So it was a bad trip. I didn't get to do anything."

AL UNSER

Photo Courtesy of the Unser Family

"To win on all those different tracks was a satisfying thing," says Al. "It really made me happy. With the dirt races and the road races, you had to be a pretty versatile driver. Back then there were guys like Foyt, my brother Bobby and Mario. There were only a few of us who could do it all. (Roger) McCluskey was pretty good at it, although he wasn't as good on the road courses. Parnelli (Jones) was another versatile driver. It would make no difference what type of car or track you were runnin' on, Parnelli could win. But winning in 1970 was really neat because I had beaten guys like Foyt, who was really a legend in dirt car racing. That made me happy. It made me feel good that I was as competitive as one of the men I worshipped."

Al started racing in 1957, when he was 17. His first race car was a modified stock car built by his father and brother Bobby, and with that car he won not only his first race but also the track Championship at Speedway Park in Albuquerque. "We called that car a super modified," Al tells the story. "But compared to today's thinking, it was like a jalopy. Anyway. we went out there and won the first race I was ever in. I cleaned house. In fact, they split the season in half because I was so many points ahead they decided to end the season and start a new season. And I won that one, too!"

"It was only because of Bobby," he continues, "who taught me a lot, and my father, who gave me the opportunity to race. I think basically, when I first started it was

■ "You hear through the years how Penske must be a man that rules with an iron hand, that if you say a bad word he scolds you and gets you down. But he doesn't do that. He does it with much finesse instead. I don't know where he comes from or how he does it, but Penske gets things done. He has that drive to him that reflects to his people but he does it with so much finesse. I mean, I can feel it within myself.

"Penske is sharp. He gets it done. He gets people to produce. When the going gets rough, it never shows with him. His people and Penske himself just keep going. It's the darndest thing. Through the years I had always heard that the rougher it gets for Penske, the more and harder he'll work. And it is that way. I guarantee you he never backs off."

141

"That's me (#56), May 5, 1957. The guy lost the left front wheel. I had just started racing Easter Sunday, 1957."

AL UNSER

Photo Courtesy of the Unser Family

just a point that it was the only thing I knew. I had three older brothers that were all racing and I liked it. I liked working on the cars. So it was just something automatically for me to do and I have not regretted it in any way. Racing has been good to me. Its a hard sport, a demanding sport. I love it."

By the middle of teenaged Al's first season of racing his success had made him unpopular, and he learned right away that racing can be a very tough sport. "The other guys were starting to block me and pull some pretty bad deals on me so Daddy got mad. He and Bobby went to Amarillo, bought a car and brought it back to Albuquerque and Bobby started running with me. It made a different story out of it. All of a sudden I had my brother helping me, and he was a lot more talented and experienced than I was. It was neat! We'd run first and second almost every night. We ended the BS out there. It became a point of who had the biggest pit crews!"

"This is at Pikes Peak in 1959. That was a very bad year. This is when they caught me the day before qualifying because I was only 20 years old. And they wouldn't let me run. And my father, trying to build up my morale, I guess, because I was very bitter and very unhappy—I'd run all of practice and all that—and the night before qualifying is when they caught me.

"I never got along with the people at Pikes Peak, because I guess I was a young kid that probably wasn't the easiest person to get along with. I guess I was a snotty young man, I don't know. But I didn't get along with them up there, and it started from this day of them catching me when I was 20 years old and they thought it was really funny. And it really was a heartbreaker. This was my dad's car that Bobby was going to run, with the Jaguar in it. In fact, this car is at the Indianapolis Motor Speedway. It's supposed to someday go in a museum, I don't know. But then Bobby got out of this car and into his own car, that I was running. See, I wasn't gonna run this car and Dad put my name on it, and all that. I don't know why—just to build my morale up, but it didn't do any good."

AL UNSER

Photo Courtesy of the Unser Family

Photo by George Shellenberger

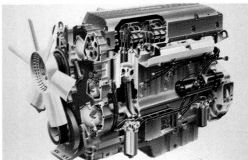

"This had to be Bobby running the car, otherwise I wouldn't have done this. I crewed for him sometimes."

AL UNSER

Photo Courtesy of the Unser Family

Photo by Mike Griffith

"This was a '59 or '60 and due to a guy named Bill Stroppe, in California, who worked for Ford Motor Company on the racing side of it. So Ford decided, when the Ford Falcon came out, to do an endurance run with about 30 cars to cover every Federal highway in the United States. So, out of the 30, Louie (right) and I were partners, and we covered the Pennsylvania Turnpike. And our job was a mileage run—totally mileage for fuel economy. And we would run the whole Pennsylvania Turnpike every day. I never got so tired of a turnpike in all my life. Never in my life. They paid me $500, the most money I'd ever made. I was tickled to death."

AL UNSER

Photo Courtesy of the Unser Family

"This is when I was building my super modified, the #56 car. and this is with a Pontiac engine. And we kept blowing it and finally put a Chevy in it. In fact, I took the engine out of the Pikes Peak car I wrecked and transferred that engine into my super modified because my bother Louie had built that Chevy engine."

AL UNSER

Photo Courtesy of the Unser Family

A racewinner from the start, Al was soon spreading his wings, racing Modifieds and Sprint cars in New Mexico, Colorado, Arizona, California, and elsewhere in the southwest. He competed at Pike's Peak for the first time in 1960 and finished second to brother Bobby. He was married to high school sweetheart Wanda Jespersen in 1958 and for a while, shared with Bobby the responsibility of running their father's repair shop and garage. Ultimately Bobby and Al argued and dissolved their partnership, leaving Bobby to run the shop and Al to take over the wrecking yard on the opposite side of the westbound road out of Albuquerque.

With the help of his father, Al got into the towing and wrecking business in 1961, continuing to race around the country, often with the smallest of change in his pocket. There were threadbare trips to the west coast, eastward to Florida, into the midwest, and, of course, to Pike's Peak in Colorado. In 1964 he made a breakthrough, beating Bobby for the first time at Pike's Peak. Driving Vince Conze's lighweight, titanium-bodied, Offy-powered machine, Al scored his first win at the Peak in record time.

"This is Speedway Park, Albuquerque, New Mexico. I must have won the Feature or the Main. And this is the car I built based on the ECCA car."

AL UNSER

Photo Courtesy of the Unser Family

"This is at Pueblo, Colorado, I (#56) went there several times. At that time, this was a good way to learn racing, very much so. It taught you how to be very aggressive—Sprint cars. It taught you how to work traffic and figure out the race tracks. And it flat taught you . . . you had to be very aggressive but if you crashed you were on the sidelines. And it used to be very, very good training."

AL UNSER

Photo Courtesy of the Unser Family

Photo by Leroy Byers

Photo by Leroy Byers

"This is Pueblo, Colorado, 1962, Bobby (#92) and me. I built that car, number 56. That was what they called the old ECCA car (#92). And this Sprint car was a very famous race car in its day. And this car (#56) basically is copied after this one (#92). But a lot of changes were made, because I used a different suspension, and everything, but the measurements were all the same on where the motor sits and how high it sits and all that.

"It took me a while to get the car to work, but it did, very much so. What caused this car to be built was that I couldn't get a ride. Nobody would give me a ride. So, I went down and borrowed the money from the bank to build this car. It had to be '61 when this car was built. I raced it until the beginning of '64 and then I sold it. And then I started running for Frank Arciero.

"I tell you what it was. When I won Pikes Peak, I decided not to run any more local tracks, to try to step up and go after better things."

AL UNSER

Photo Courtesy of the Unser Family

Photo by Leroy Byers

"This is the old ECCA car that Bobby was in. I ended up with the ride. And the guy that bought the car from Ron McGowen, he was gonna take me racing; if I maintained the car, he would pay all the bills and all that. Well, I bought all the tires, I went down to Tampa, Florida and I never got a dime from him. He paid for the race car. But that's all. In other words, he never gave me any money to go down there on. I used my own money because he said that when I got back he would straighten it up with me. And to get back, I had to make the race. Otherwise I would never have been able to get back."

AL UNSER

Photo Courtesy of the Unser Family

Photo by C and R Photos

Photo by Burry Dolbeare

"This was at Pike's Peak, 1960. It was my first Pike's Peak car that I built and owned. It has a Pontiac in it. It was a hard deal. It was very cold—you can see I have a jacket on."

AL UNSER

Photo Courtesy of the Unser Family

"Denver, Colorado after the race. Bobby beat me that day and I ran second. This had to be 1960 or '61."
AL UNSER
Photo Courtesy of the Unser Family

Photo by Leroy Byers

"This is at Sacramento, California. A young punk kid! Old cloth helmet days, and all. This had to be the early '60s."
AL UNSER
Photo Courtesy of the Unser Family

"This was at Pike's Peak in 1963. I built my own car for up there. It was something I couldn't afford, but I did it anyway. I wanted to own my own car . . . well, first place, I couldn't get a ride. It took all the money I had. This day here, when I left Pikes Peak, I had something like 50 cents to my name, totally, after I paid all my bills. And I had a gas credit card so that I could get back home to Albuquerque.

"I crashed this day. And after this race at Pikes Peak in '63 I would not own my own car, no more. Because I just couldn't afford it and I could run for other people. And that's when I came back with Vince Conze and won the race the next year."

AL UNSER

"That was my place of business in Albuquerque, which is shut down now. That building still sits there. The one to the left, I tore down and I added on the front of this so you can't actually see this anymore. I could take you in there and show you where that little door is still there. Where the window is, there's a door that lifts up and down now. I laid the foundation myself with a shovel. I built that thing—I don't know how I ever could afford it. I used to nickel and dime everything.

"When I had the business, I wanted very badly to make it a success. And when I closed it, it was a success. It was just starting to take hold. But I used to work—I had a towing service, a wrecking yard and a repair shop. And I used to run my wreckers all night, myself and then work all day. It was something I worked very hard at. And when I closed it, it was a heartbreaking deal because it ... many times, I've been back in my wrecking yard, still today, everything's still there and I used to be able to tell you every car I bought and what I paid for it. It was heartbreaking to go back down through there and see all the things that I worked very hard for, that I just locked the doors because I couldn't run it and the people that I had running it were stealing more than I could ... just typical people."

AL UNSER

Photo Courtesy of the Unser Family

"This was at Speedway Park in Albuquerque. I sponsored a stock car. Unser Auto Parts was my business in Albuquerque."

AL UNSER

Photo Courtesy of the Unser Family

Above
Al Unser competing in Frank
Arciero's Lotus 19 at the October,
1964 running of the Pacific GP
at Laguna Seca.

Below
"This was Frank Harrison's car,
out of Chattanooga, Tennessee.
He owned the car. And a guy
named Jerry Eisert, he was the
chief mechanic. This was '65,
when I won the race. In '64 I
won it in Vince Conze's car."

AL UNSER

Photo Courtesy of the Unser Family

■ "I've always said
whether you're a road racer
or an oval racer, you should
be able to adapt to either
one or the other. I don't think
there should be, or that there
is, one type of driver. A race
driver should be able to run
anything. I could never understand why a guy couldn't
change his style from oval
to road racing or the other
way. When you go to any
racetrack you work at it and
learn how to change and
adapt to it. For an oval racer
who has never done any
road racing, it's hard. Bobby
and I were lucky from the
standpoint of doing Pike's
Peak. I got tied up with Frank
Arciero when I first started,
and we did some road racing
with a Lotus sports car. So
it was easier for me to adapt
than it was for some other
drivers when road racing
started coming into the
Championship. I still lay
most of what Bobby and I
have been able to do on road
courses onto Pike's Peak
because that is nothing but a
road course.

151

Taking and passing his Indianapolis 500 rookie test in
Frank Arciero's Maserati-powered racer, Al was unable
to get this car into the race.

152

"This was 1965, my rookie year at Indianapolis. I
finished ninth. When you first go to Indianapolis, it's so
confusing, being a rookie, because there's so many
things going on that I don't know whether it was what I
expected, or not. It was something that I wanted very
badly.

"They weren't going to let me take my test. I didn't have
enough experience, they said. Then Bobby (left) and
my father (center)—my father, if it wasn't for him I
would have never made it because he pushed every
day—and Foyt and a guy named Rodger Ward who
was a driver rep at that time for USAC—he went in and
vouched for me—and they finally OK'd me taking a
test. At first they said no and then they finally OK'd it
and I passed my test. And after that it was a hard, uphill
battle to make the race.

"It's funny seeing this picture with Goodyear on my
uniform.

I can't even remember that. But it was with Foyt so I
had to have a Goodyear uniform."

AL UNSER

Photo Courtesy of the Unser Family

The following year Al was at Indianapolis with a car built by his brother Louie. Bankrolled by Frank Arciero, the car was powered by a Maserati engine that didn't have the horsepower to compete with the Ford and Offenhauser engines of the time.

"First they didn't want to let me run because I didn't have enough experience," says Al. "But thanks to Rodger Ward, who was USAC drivers' representative, and my father and brother Louie, USAC finally let me take a test."

Al passed his rookie test in Arciero's car but after more than a week of practice, it was clear he wasn't going to make the field. One last, desperate attempt was made on the final day of qualifying. The over-stressed engine blew up.

"I was a very dejected and unhappy man," remembers Al. "I thought the world had come to an end, and I was sitting in the garage hanging my head between my legs. And Foyt walked in and asked me if I wanted to run his backup car. He said, 'Think about it and come over to my garage and let me know.' Well, it was real funny because he turned around and walked out of my garage, and I was right on his bumper. I mean, I was after him!"

Al took over Foyt's backup car that day, practiced it and qualified for the 500. With brother Louie doing the mechanical work on the car, he started from the last row and went on to finish ninth, four laps behind winner Jim Clark.

Says Al, "Foyt treated me so well in that deal, in getting me into the car and in teaching me. There were several people in his organization that did not want me in the car, because I was a rookie. They were saying, 'Why would he put a rookie in his car when there are drivers lined up at the door trying

"I think it's easier now for the road racer to adapt to the type of oval racing we have today than it is going the other way, from ovals to road courses. People say this one or that one must be easy, but they're both hard. In oval racing you have to be very exact and the cars run very quick. On road courses you can make more mistakes and get away with it.

Al ready to qualify for his first Indy 500 flanked by (left to right) Louie Unser, Bill Ansted, car-owner AJ Foyt, and George Bignotti.

Photo by Bob Tronolone

153

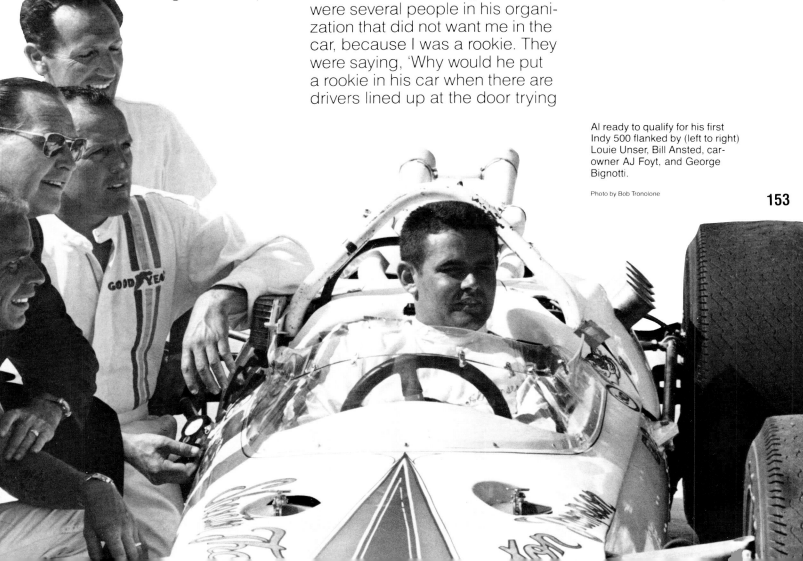

to get into that car?' It amazes me still today that Foyt did that for me. He must've had some foresight, looking at me and being able to say well, he's got some talent. It just amazed me that he gave me that opportunity. It still does today.

"We went out and ran the car, and he sat down in his garage and drew out the racetrack and told me where to back off and where to get on the gas. 'You do that,' he says, 'and you'll make the race.' So I went back out and ran a couple of laps. He only let me run about five laps or so. It wasn't very many, and I got within striking distance of making the show. I think I was half-a mile-an-hour away from making it so Foyt just brought me in, took the car back to the garage, fueled it up and said, 'You're ready to qualify.' I tell you, I had never been so scared in all my life.

"Then he just set me down again and explained to me what to do. He said, 'You just do what I tell you and you'll make the race.' And I did. That's just exactly what happened. It was down to the nitty-gritty and it was a great feeling to be able to do that. The Speedway has been good to me, you know. Through my whole career, it's been one of those racetracks that has been good to me."

Driving for Frank Harrison's small team, Al took part in most of the remaining championship races of 1965. In July he won again at Pike's Peak and planned to drive

During most of 1965 and in the initial '66 event, Al drove this Frank Harrison-owned car tended by chief mechanic Jerry Eisert (left).

154

for Harrison again in 1966. "But Andy Granatelli called me and wanted to know if I'd be interested in driving a Lotus at the (Indianapolis Motor) Speedway. Well, that didn't take much thought. I jumped at that."

The Lotus team had won the 500 in 1965 with Scotsman Jim Clark so that in his second year at the Speedway, Al was teammate to the previous year's winner. Engine and transmission problems kept Al from qualifying until the second weekend, however, and despite recording the sixth fastest qualifying time he had to start among the tailenders. He quickly moved up through the field and was running with the leaders late in the race when his car's suspension failed and he crashed, without injury.

Al's job with STP and Lotus was for that race alone so he was out of work once the race was over. At the following evening's victory banquet, Rodger Ward, 1959 and 1962 Indy 500 winner, made the surprising announcement that he was retiring from the sport. The next day Al was chasing hard after Ward's vacant seat. "I didn't know Ward was going to retire until the banquet, and I was down at (George) Bignotti's doorstep at eight o'clock the next morning, before he even got there."

"What's happened with Sprint car racing, Midgets, dirt track racing—whatever you want to call it—is that those cars are now entirely separated from Indycars. An upright dirt car is completely different from the type of rear-engined cars we run today. Twenty or 30 years ago, they were alike. If you showed talent in a Midget or Sprint car or Dirt car you could go to Indianapolis, and if you had talent, you could do well. But being able to run one of those cars today means nothing as far as running an Indycar.

"I still say that a Sprint car will teach you so much, as they did with Al Junior. They teach you throttle control and quick thinking because a Sprint car is a very fast-acting car. You have to be very sharp mind-wise and reaction-wise to keep up with them through traffic and being able to learn how to charge through a group of cars while using your head and not losing control or knowing where you're at. It's really a good teaching ground, but towards teaching you how to run a speedway car, it doesn't do it anymore.

155

Jim Clark's teammate, Al Unser, ensconced in his STP Lotus during practice for the 1966 Indy 500.

Al on the Hanford straight during the USAC 200 in
October, 1967.

Photo by Bob Tronolo

At Sacramento in October, 1967, Al judges how long a
walk it will be back to the garage after losing an engine.

Photo by Bob Tronolo

Bignotti remains to this day the most successful chief mechanic in the history of Indycar racing (with 84 wins) and at the time ran the team owned by Texas oilman John Mecom. Bignotti agreed that Al would be a good choice to replace the retiring Ward, but Mecom preferred Sprint car star Larry Dickson. So, the team ran both men at the next race. "We went to Milwaukee and I made the race and did alright and we just went from race to race for a while," explains Al. "I didn't know what the deal was all about and for a while I didn't even have my name on the car. Then Dickson decided to pull himself out because he didn't feel he had the experience to do it right. Finally, they put my name on the car at one of the races. I asked George if I was hired yet. 'Well,' he says, 'I put your name on the car, didn't I?'

"So that was the way it got started for me with the main teams. It was neat. You could never plan it that way. They weren't beating on my door but I sure was beating on theirs."

A somber Al Unser during Indy's "Merry Month of May," 1968.

Regardless of the angle, Al's practice crash prior to the '68 Indy 500 resulted in a less-than-pristine race car.

There's no connection between how a Sprint car feels and an Indycar feels.

"So a man that has come along in an upright car today, unless he's still young, it's going to be a waste of time for him to get into a rear-engined car. His percentage of making it is very low compared to a man who has come up through Formula Fords and Super Vees because those cars lean more toward the handling characteristics of an Indycar.

"Regardless of whether it's the wide tires or wings, I don't think a front-engined, upright car gives you the same feel as a rear-engined car. It's just a totally different feel and you run the two different types of car in a totally different way. I've never run a Sprint car with a wing on it so I don't know what they feel like. But when I talk to guys that drive Sprint cars today, they say you just go down in there and throw it sideways and you get in the throttle all the way. But they still drift those cars whereas with a rear-engined

In 1967 and '68, Al drove for Al Retzloff's team, scoring a string of seconds in '67 and winning his first Indycar-type race in '68. With George Bignotti taking over the job of chief mechanic, Al became a regular winner, and in 1969 Bignotti and he moved together to the new Vel's Parnelli Jones team. Al missed the Indy 500 that year, breaking a leg in a motorcycle accident inside the Speedway's grounds a few days prior to the race. But he came back to win five races later in the year, finishing second to Mario Andretti in the national Championship. In 1970 and '71, aboard Bignotti's four-cam Ford-powered VPJ cars (there were turbocharged Ford, rear-engined, Lola-based Colts for the paved tracks, and for the dirt tracks, normally aspirated Fords in the team's front-engined Grant King cars), Al was the man to beat. In 1970 he won ten of 18 races, the Indianapolis 500 included, and took the national Championship. The following year, with dirt track races removed from the Championship, Al continued to dominate, winning five of the season's first six races, including a second successive Indianapolis 500. In the second half of the year, he failed to finish a single race, however, and faded to fourth in the Championship, which was taken by teammate Joe Leonard.

Al pilots his Retzloff asphalt racer through Riversides's Turn 6 during the Rex Mays 300 in 1968.

Al slides his Retzloff dirt racer through Sacramento's third turn on September 29, 1968.

car you don't drift. You might to a certain degree on a road course, but you'll never see it on an oval. The speeds are so much greater, and it's a completely different feel.

"When I used to run dirt cars I had to change my way of thinking when I got out of a rear-engined car and into a front-engined Dirt car. I had to change my actions toward the car so that I could respond to the car. It's a different deal, as it is when you run stock cars. It's the same thing. You have to change your way of thinking as you do when you go from a road course to an oval."

Al tackles Hanford in his new Vel's Parnelli Jones racer,
April 13, 1969.

160

"Oh my gosh, I don't even remember this! It's Mario
(Andretti), a Firestone guy—there's four of us in the
boat. It's the infield lake at Hanford. We were there
testing and somebody had a boat and we took it for a
ride."

AL UNSER

Al poses with the race queen at Indianapolis Raceway
Park .

"This was at the Hoosier Hundred in 1969. That's Bobby's race car and Mike Mosley (center), Bobby (right) and myself. That was right before the start of the race."

AL UNSER

The front row for the 1970 Indianapolis 500: (right to left) Al Unser, Johnny Rutherford and AJ Foyt.

On his way to his first Indianapolis 500 victory, Al races
Mark Donohue down Indy's main straight.

Photo by Bob Tronolc

Photo by Bob Tronolc

"This is in the (1970 Indianapolis 500) winner's circle the first year. You know, its funny, it was neat. It was something I wanted very much. You ask me now, since I've won three others, it's kind of hard. But your first one's always neat because it shows that you can win, and it opens a lot of doors that were never open before, taking advantage of everything that goes on in racing. This whole month of May, we were the fastest car, so it's one of those deals, we knew that if we finished, we'd win. Which we did, and there was no problem. When it's right, it's right."

AL UNSER

Photo Courtesy of the Unser Family

162

"That was taken in 1970 when I came into town for the (post-Indy) parade. 'Congratulations, Al. What do you say to a naked lady?' I would like to know!"

AL UNSER

Photo Courtesy of the Unser Family

Three-wheeling through Sacramento's third turn on his way to victory. Al won all five Championship dirt car events on the '70 Champ car schedule, culminating in USAC's national Championship.

Photo by Bob Tronolone

"This was in the Rudy Hoerr Ford stock car that I drove at either DuQuoin or Springfield. I won a couple races with this car, but we didn't win as many as we should've. We had many of them won and things always broke— broke the motor or something would happen. Rudy and Annie Hoerr owned that car. They still race today with their son."

AL UNSER

Photo Courtesy of the Unser Family

"This is in 1971 with the Johnny Lightning (Vel's Parnelli ones Colt-Ford)."

L UNSER

oto Courtesy of the Unser Family

"This is at Indianapolis—getting the checkered flag in '71 (for the second, successive time)."

AL UNSER

Photo Courtesy of the Unser Family

165

"This is in '71 when I won the race (Indianapolis 500). Drinking the milk … when you win that race, you'll drink anything they hand you. It makes no difference, you could care less! It's a tradition that they have, and that's just the way it goes. It's neat, what they do."

AL UNSER

Photo Courtesy of the Unser Family

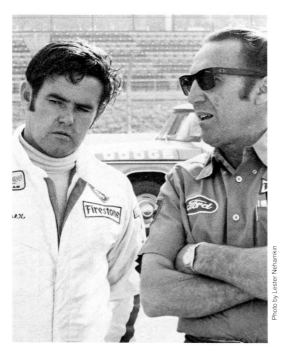

Photo by Lester Nehamkin

"Ontario, California. George Bignotti ... and I probably trying to figure out what the hell's wrong with the car. This was '71 with the Johnny Lightning car, and at that time the car was becoming very obsolete ... trying to figure out why it wouldn't run quicker than it would."

AL UNSER

Photo Courtesy of the Unser Family

Those were times of rapid change both in automobile racing and in Al's own life. A few months before winning his first Indy 500 he closed down his wrecking yard and towing service, leaving the large wrecking yard dormant behind his house, as it remains today. Before winning his second Indy 500, Al had separated from Wanda. Divorce loomed on the horizon.

Meanwhile, the VPJ team switched from Ford to Offenhauser engines after AJ Foyt bought the exclusive rights to the Ford engine. The change didn't affect Joe Leonard, who won three of that year's slim schedule of ten Championship races. Al finished a rather distant second at Indianapolis and won the Pocono 500 before being penalized one lap for passing under the yellow flag. As it was, he was unable to record a single win that year, the first time in four racing seasons Al had gone winless. During this time he continued to race dirt cars and stock cars in separate USAC Championship series, there often winning a race or two each year.

Photo by Bob Tronolone

Unwatched by almost everyone, Al races Mike Mosley down the Phoenix straight in the unloved '72 version of a Parnelli-Offy.

"This is at Springfield in 1973. Grant King built the car in '72. And then, over the winter from that year to this year, Bignotti changed a lot of the working parts on the car—changed quite a bit—and that's when it really started to work."

AL UNSER

Photo Courtesy of the Unser Family

Photo by Dennis Torres

"The #22 car was Greg Weld. There was no contest to me outrunning him, you know. I won the race that day. It was the Hoosier Hundred in 1973.

"The Hoosier Hundred used to be a big deal: the biggest paying race we had, except for Indianapolis."
AL UNSER

The unloved '73 version of the Parnelli-Offy at the 1973 running of the Indy 500.

"This is was at Pocono in '73. I hit the wall very hard that day. I lost it and hit the wall. I think I just hit the bump down there in Turn One where you're really running fast. It was at the first of the race, the first 20 or 30 laps, something like that.

"This was a very bad car. I don't know why. If I knew, I could have fixed it. It just … it was owned by Vels Parnelli, and Maurice Phillippe was the designer, and we just never could make this car work. It did weird things and this was one of those weird days.

"Karen came there. This was her first race with me. She went to the hospital with me."

AL UNSER

Photo Courtesy of the Unser Family

170

"This was at Michigan with the Viceroy (Offy-powered) Eagle in 1974."

AL UNSER

Photo Courtesy of the Unser Family

"This is with the go karts, Al and I. He looks like a little girl! We used to go out every weekend and run go karts. That's how he got started.

"Everybody kept saying, 'He's gonna be three times better than you.' And I always used to say that I hoped he was, but one step at a time. I always wanted him to, but I never said he would be what he is today. Because it would be unfair. I don't believe in that. It's just like in anything. You might learn so much and then you just taper off. How many people do that in everything—in football, in every day work—and they never get any better. Well, Al always progressed very rapidly and he was good at it, if he set his mind to it. And that's one thing I had trouble with him doing, is making sure he did it—focused in."

AL UNSER

Al at speed during the 1974 running of the Hoosier Hundred.

Photo Courtesy of the Unser Family

Aboard Indianapolis-type cars, the years 1972-75 were slim ones for Al. In an attempt to restrain speeds which had escalated rapidly in 1971, '72 and '73, USAC implemented limits on fuel consumption and then turbo boost pressure. At the same time, engine reliability became a giant headache for many teams, Vel's Parnelli Jones among them. Pressed for sponsorship, the VPJ outfit even stopped building its own cars, buying Eagles from Dan Gurney in 1974 and 1975. In fact, Al ran only half the Indycar schedule in 1975 as the team focused on Formula 5000 road racing, utilizing stock-block-based Chevrolet engines. Teamed in F5000 with Mario Andretti, he won a race in the rain at Road Atlanta and finished a close third in the Championship behind Brian Redman and Andretti. The following year, Al finished second to Redman in the F5000 Championship and won the final race of the year at Riverside.

"This was at Syracuse, New York, a dirt race, in 1974. That's Karen (to Al's immediate left) and my daughter Debbie. I was very tired that day. I thought I was out of shape because I got out of the car and I was *so* tired. Mario was laying on the ground. High, high humidity: It was like 90, 95 percent and the heat was the same. I've never been through anything like that. It was *hot*."

AL UNSER

Photo Courtesy of the Unser Family

Photo by Dennis Torres

By this time the VPJ team had taken a fresh look at Indycar racing and had produced a ground-breaking new car based on the Formula One car the team had developed for Mario Andretti. The new Parnelli Indycar was the first to be powered by a Cosworth engine, and it was Al who not only debuted the new car and engine at Phoenix in November, 1975, but also scored the first Indycar victory for a Cosworth engine in the 1976 Pocono 500. He won two more races that year. With new teammate Danny Ongais, Al was often a front-runner in 1977. He won only one race in '77, how-ever—the California 500—and after nine years with VPJ, Al decided it was time to move on. For the '78 season he joined Jim Hall's new Indycar team.

Hall's team had raced the amazing Chaparral Can-Am and endurance racing cars in the 1960s and, in partnership with Carl Haas' team, had fielded Brian Redman's ultra-successful F5000 Lolas from 1973-76. A new Chaparral Indycar was planned, but in the interim Hall was going to run a new Lola chassis. It had been nine years since Lola Cars had designed and built an Indycar, so it wasn't surprising that the new car was competent but not very quick. Then, before going to Indi-anapolis that spring, Al survived a giant crash at Texas World Speed-way. Nevertheless, he qualified fifth fastest for the 500 and, helped by good fuel mileage, ran strongly in the race. His rivals began falling by the wayside or were forced to slow down to conserve fuel. Ulti-mately, Al won the '78 Indy 500 by just under nine seconds over Tom Sneva in one of Roger Penske's cars.

■ *"I had several offers through the years (to race Formula One). I just didn't want to do the travelling and there were so many races over here to run that I elected to stay over here. I always felt that if I was going to do F1, then I'd have to do it all the way. You cannot split yourself, because those guys are not asleep. You're not going over to pick on some cripples. It would take several years to learn the courses and to learn their way of racing. It's a different world and different cars.*

"I could've driven for Lotus way back. I talked to (chief engineer) Patrick Head about doing some testing for Williams (three-time F1 Champions). Then there was McLaren (also three-time F1 Champions). I could've gone with McLaren at one time. They were all good teams and good offers, but I just didn't want to do it."

173

The '75 version of Vel's Parnelli Jones Racing unloved
Eagle-Offy with Al at the wheel during the Cal 500 at
Ontario Motor Speedway.

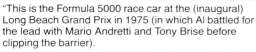

"This is the Formula 5000 race car at the (inaugural) Long Beach Grand Prix in 1975 (in which Al battled for the lead with Mario Andretti and Tony Brise before clipping the barrier).

"(Although teammate Mario Andretti was participating in the F5000 series as a tune-up for Formula One,) I had no intentions of going over and running F1. I didn't like the travelling and I didn't want to go over there and live. And there was all the racing in the world over here that I wanted to do. So I could care less about going over there. I had many offers to go over there and run and I wouldn't do it"

AL UNSER

■ "When I first started racing out here in Albuquerque, I wanted to win at the local tracks. Of course, I used to go watch the dirt races down in Phoenix on the old fairgrounds and I went to Sacramento and places like that and naturally, I wanted to do it. It was something I wanted to do but whether I could do it or not and have the breaks to get into the game, I had no idea. Naturally, every year when Indianapolis was run I was glued to the radio, you know, and I said someday I would be there. But that was just a kid talking. But I wanted to do it, yeah."

175

BOSCH salutes Al Unser on his fourth Indy 500 Victory

In 1987 Bosch spark plugs helped Al Unser win the Indy 500. Just like they helped Ray Harroun win the first Indy in 1911.

For Al Unser, 1987 marked his record-tying fourth Indy 500 win running on Bosch Spark Plugs. At Bosch, we're proud to be part of this great Unser family tradition of winning.

We pay special tribute to Al Sr., and the entire Unser family who have over the years helped us prove again the performance and reliability of Bosch Spark Plugs in the great sport of auto racing.

BOSCH

Robert Bosch Corporation
Sales Group

Photo by Dennis Torres

"Wow, this is too much! This was in '75. I enjoyed running in the dirt. I had a very good race car and a very good team, so it all worked together and I enjoyed it. This car here won every race it was ever entered but one race—it might be two. But it was a remarkable history to the car because it just automatically started winning from the day it was built. And the last Hoosier Hundred race when I finished second, I should have won that race, but I had a little mix-up on the last lap. I was passing the guy that won it and he intentionally hit me. But that's racing.

"I quit running that car in '75."

AL UNSER

Photo Courtesy of the Unser Family

"This is Jim Chapman (right) who was the chief mechanic and organizer for Vel and Parnelli. He's a good man. And Mario and I . Mario and I always got along. He never bothered me, and I never bothered him. When we were in trouble with the cars, we helped each other. But if we were not, we never told each other what we were doing."

AL UNSER

Photo Courtesy of the Unser Family

The master reporter of American auto racing, Chris Economaki, interviews Al following his November, 1976 win at Phoenix's USAC 150.

Photo by Bob Tronolone

At the wheel of his VPJ 6C, Al leads Gordon Johncock and AJ Foyt on his way to victory in the 1977 Cal 500 Ontario Motor Speedway

Photo by Bob Tronolone

178

At the '76 running of the Indy 500, Al, in his Parnelli-Cosworth VPJ 6B, debuted the Cosworth engine to this hallowed hall of American auto racing. In June, he earned the first Indycar win for the Cosworth name with his victory at the Pocono 500.

Photo by Bob Tronolone

"This is the Pocono Race in 1976, the Schaefer trophy. It was a good day. I win that race again, I'm gonna take that trophy home with me. The last year I won it they never gave me a trophy. Nothing would they give me. Schaefer pulled out ... a couple of years before when I won it they gave me a very nice trophy: cups and a big plaque—silver. It was neat! And then the last year that I won it, they didn't ever give me any trophy. I have nothing to show but pictures of winning that race."

AL UNSER

Photo Courtesy of the Unser Family

Photo by Dennis Torres

From Left to Right: Tim Solso/Vice-President, Cummins Engine Company, Inc.; Jim Henderson/President, Cummins Engine Company, Inc.; Al Unser/Driver; Roger Penske/Owner, Penske Racing; Charlie Bumb/Vice-President, Cummins Engine Company, Inc.

From Left to Right: Mr. Knut "Ben" Bendixen, V.P./Robert Bosch Corporation, his wife Ilse, Al Unser, Virginia Barnes and Bruce Barnes, President of Barnes Management.

Driving the Chapparal Racing Lola in the 1978 Indian-apolis 500, Al captured win number three at the Brickyard.

Al's third win at Indy presaged a good season wherein he finished a close second to Tom Sneva in the national Championship. Rarely a race leader with the Lola, he was a frequent finisher among the top five and achieved an apparent impossibility by also winning the Pocono and California 500s. It was the first and, thus far, the last time that one man has accomplished the feat of winning all three Indycar 500 mile races in a single season.

Meanwhile, work was beginning on the new Chaparral Indycar. Designed by the brilliant young English engineer John Barnard, who had reworked the Parnelli F1 car into the successful Cosworth-engined Indycar of 1976-78, the Chaparral appeared for the first time at Indianapolis in May, 1979. Without benefit of any testing, Al qualified the "Yellow Submarine" on the outside of the front row and dominated the race until stopped by a transmission failure. After that remarkable debut, the car proved a little less competitive in most of the remaining races, although at the last race of the year, Al took the Chaparral to a dominant flag-to-flag win.

A few weeks later, Al let it be known he was leaving the Chaparral outfit, surprising news to many as it looked as if the team was getting its act together. Indeed, in 1980 Johnny Rutherford was to win both the Indy 500 and the national Championship aboard the "Yellow Submarine." Al never liked to

discuss his departure from Hall's team with the press, but the fact is that he was joined by most other members of Hall's team in leaving at the end of the '79 season.

"I just didn't like the way things were being done," he says. "That entire time (with the Chaparral in 1979) we only tested one time and that was before the last race at Phoenix. Nobody in the team was very happy. John Barnard left. Franz Weis, the engine man, went to do his own thing. We all agreed that things weren't being done in the right way."

Al took the gamble of joining Bobby Hillin's team. A Texas oil dealer who was an amateur sports car racer, Hillin had run an Indycar team for a couple of years before deciding to build his own cars and hire a top-line driver. For three years Hillin and Al went racing together in Hillin's succession of cars called Longhorns. Although there were times when the cars were fast, often the Longhorns were off the pace. What was most important to Al was the fact that Hillin put everything into making the team successful. He spent a great deal of his own money, searched the world for the best people, and tried to test his cars rigorously in the best tradition of the top teams like Penske Racing.

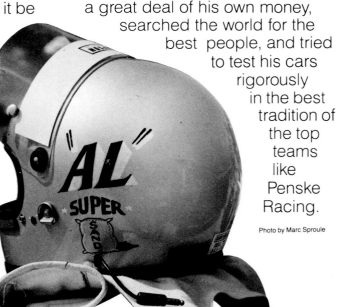

Photo by Marc Sproule

Having won the first two legs of the '78 Triple Crown, Indy and Pocono, they were on to Al by the running of the third and final leg, the Cal 500.

The field takes the green following a caution during the final stages of Ontario's Cal 500, and Al takes the lead.

(From left to right) Karen Unser, Sandy and Jim Hall will Al across the finish line as he takes the win of the Cal 500 and the 1978 Triple Crown.

183

Photos by Marc Sproule

Karen greets Al in victory circle. "The Ontario 500, '78, that did the Triple Crown, that race right there. You wonder why. I couldn't make the car work at any other race tracks but long tracks. And it wouldn't work very good then. But the same old thing, Lady Luck and the good Lord upstairs rode with us and we were able to win 'em."

AL UNSER

Al contests Watkins Glen in th
new Chapparal 2K, which
presented at the '79 Indy 50
running away with the race b
fore being sidelined with m
chanical difficultie

"I could never fault Hillin for the enthusiasm and honesty he brought to his race team," reflects Al. "He wanted to make it work. He tried as hard as any man I've ever known in racing. He deserved to succeed but it just never did happen."

Al was unable to win a race for Hillin, creating the longest winless stretch in his Indycar career. There were new cars every year and modified versions in the middle of some seasons. In July, 1981, midway through Al's happy but frustrating tenure with Hillin, he found himself clear of a decimated field in the inaugural Michigan 500, only to have his engine blow up with barely 100 miles to go. In August, 1980, at Watkins Glen, Al led from brother Bobby, lost the lead to his brother, then crashed while leaving the pits after a stop for fuel and tires. It was an atypical mistake for Al, the result of a tricky turbo setup designed to work on the racecourse but less effective under acceleration in the tight, downhill-and-turning Glen pit lane. It was typical, however, of the bad luck which dogged Al and the Longhorn team over those three years.

In his first year with Hillin, 1980, Al pilots a Longhorn LR01 at Indy.

At Phoenix, Al and Kare cele brate Al's finally scoring a victory with the Chapparal in the las race of the '79 season, only two weeks before Al left the team

■ "I wanted Al Junior to race. When we started in go karts, it was a father—me—pushing it. I think I got more of a charge out of it than he did. It was just one of those deals that I wanted him to do and we did it. Until Al started coming around and showing some interest, it was just me. You know, how can an eight-year-old kid know what he wants? It comes down to the father and mother pushing it, whatever it is, whether it's singing, sewing or whatever.

"So the boy showed some talent as he has in everything he's done. He's been one of those exceptional students at anything he's done. Many things seem to come easy to him and racing was just one of those things. I had no idea he would turn out to be the driver that he has turned out to be. Everything was a stepping-stone for him, from karts to Sprint cars to Super Vees and then to the Can-Am and Indycars.

Near the end of the 1980 season, Al ran a Can-Am sports car race at Laguna Seca. Driving a car called a Frissbee in his only Can-Am race of the year, he won the race, beating the likes of 1981 Formula One World Champion, Keke Rosberg, French F1 star Patrick Tambay, Geoff Brabham, and the top young American road racers of the times: Bobby Rahal, Danny Sullivan, et al. The following year he started the Can-Am season with Paul Newman's team, teamed with the Italian up-and-comer Teo Fabi. Al and the team did not enjoy each other's company, however, and after five races he pulled out (his place taken by Bobby Rahal) and concentrated on his Indycar season with Hillin.

Another thing that was occupying Al's time and mind during this period was the arrival of his son, Al Junior in the national automobile racing theater. After Al was divorced from Wanda, Al Junior and his sisters, Mary and Debbie, lived with their mother. Around the time that Al and Wanda separated, Al Junior started racing go karts. He continued to do so, the little machines tuned and run out of his father's shop. Into his teenaged years, Al Junior decided he was enjoying racing karts so much, he moved back to his dad's house. During this time, Al had been courting Karen Barnes, a bright, attractive young woman he had met while racing in the Midwest, and in 1976 they married.

"This is at Laguna Seca, California in 1980 when I won my first Can-Am (for Brad Frisselle Racing). This was the Formula 5000 car with the Can-Am body on it."

AL UNSER

Photo Courtesy of the Unser Family

"This was in 1980 at Milwaukee Wisconsin. I was leading the race that day—there's (lower left corner) Johnny Rutherford. That's when I left Jim Hall and went with Hillin . The right front wheel fell off. What happened was the pins were too long and the wheel finally set in and loosened a nut and it finally came off. I had the race won. I was long gone, and they couldn't catch me. And that was another one of those deals I should've had

AL UNSER

Photo Courtesy of the Unser Family

"This is Karen and me on a motorcycle ride in '80 up in Colorado with Wally Dallenbach—the Colorado 500."

AL UNSER

"How can anybody know that anyone can step up to the next stage of something and be able to carry it? It's easy to see someone out running go karts and say he's good and all that—and Al did run good in karts. He smoked'em! But you know we had things right, good equipment. It was no contest. So, like I say, you can't tell what will come with the next step.

"As it turned out, Al did a tremendous job when he moved into Sprint cars. He amazed me. I just couldn't believe that an 18-year-old kid could do what he could. Then when he moved into Super Vees he showed potential there. With a little training and a little coaching, he started responding. The

"This is Louie and me at Riverside. I did a Toyota celebrity race out there in 1982. Louie is a very, very talented engine builder. He was always, I think a much smarter engine builder than he was a race car driver. We used to call him, "Screwy Louie" because he was a good driver but he just basically never did use good judgment for some reason. I think that he would've, eventually, come out of that— Bobby was like that, somewhat, but not nearly like Louie and then finally Bobby settled down and started winning. And I think Louie would've, too, if MS wouldn't have got him because he was a good race driver. He was just too brave."

AL UNSER

Photo Courtesy of the Unser Family

Al in Hillin's Longhorn LR02 at Milwaukee, 1981.

190

"This is at Portland, Oregon in 1983. There's Rick (right), Penske (back to camera), and Al when he was running for Coors with Galles."

AL UNSER

Photo Courtesy of the Unser Family

Having raced karts regularly and well, in 1978, the year his father won the Triple Crown, Al Junior started racing Sprint cars. He continued to progress through Super Vees into the Can-Am, winning the Can-Am Championship in 1982 at 20 years of age. Through this time his dad was always there, worrying over his son, watching him, advising him. For so many years Al had lived in brother Bobby's shadow. Even after winning Indy two years in a row and then a third time, Al happily permitted his more loquacious older brother to dominate the stage. Not until Al Junior appeared in the public eye in company with his father as instructor, teacher and confidant, did Al's personality begin to be exposed to, and known by, the world outside.

In August of 1982, during the last of his three years with Bobby Hillin's team, Al and the Unser family were struck by tragedy when Al's daughter Debbie was killed in a dunebuggy accident. Al was in Milwaukee when he heard the news, qualifying for the following day's 200 mile race at the Wisconsin State Fair Park. Hillin immediately scratched the car from the field, and Al and Karen flew home that night. Debbie was 21, dark-haired, and very attractive. Al took her death hard.

Al contests Riverside's Air Ca 500 in Hillin's Longhorn LR03 1982. This was the last yea Al was to drive for Hillin

Photo by Marc Sproule

Little more than a month later, Hillin told Al that he was going to have to close down his race team. The oil industry was in bad shape and Hillin had spent a small fortune trying to establish an Indy-car team. The news was not very surprising. Right away, Al started talking with the top team owners in the business: Roger Penske, Pat Patrick and a man named Jerry Forsythe who had a new team that was said to be the English Indycar builder March Engineering's "factory" effort for 1983.

"I just weighed it all out," says Al, "and decided that I would go with Penske. In the first place, he was more—the two teams I was really debating about were Patrick's and Penske's—and well, Roger was more exact. Patrick was worried about different things along the way and Penske was unconcerned about that. He just said, 'Let's think it over.' I asked him to go and talk to Derrick Walker (Penske's race team boss) and to the crew and make sure they were happy to have me. I really wouldn't want to go to any team—either stay with a team or go with a another team—that is not happy with me.

kid just totally responded to what I would tell him. Of course, after the Super Vees he stepped into the Can-Am cars and did the job and now he's shown that he can do it in Speedway cars as well. There are no more stepping-stones. He's won some Indycar races and the next step for him is to win the big races and the Championship. Eventually, some way, he'll do that. He has that knack, whatever it is. It's nothing I've taught him.''

Photo by Bob Tronolone

In 1987, Al presented the Porsche Indycar to the American racing fan at Laguna Seca.

Photo by Dan Bianchi

Photo by Art Flores

Driving for Roger Penske, Al broke his 37-race losing streak with a victory at Cleveland in 1983 and went on to win the national Championship that year.

"I said that to Penske because of Bobby having been there. Bobby had a very hard time with certain people on the team, so I wanted to make sure they were happy to have me, not just because Penske was going to hire me. I wanted them to want me on their own. I had already been through a deal with the March Can-Am car where (Paul) Newman hired me and the crew didn't want me and I didn't want that to happen again. Of course, Penske came back right away and said it's OK. Then I went and talked to Derrick myself because I really wanted to make sure he and the crew were happy with me."

In fact, the relationship between Al and Penske's team has grown very strong. Into his sixth year with Penske Racing, Al has two Championships under his belt (1983 and 1985) and one Indy 500 win (1987). Since 1985, Al has occupied the rather curious role of the team's "backup driver." Around Penske's garages you'll often hear Al affectionately referred to as, "The Old Man" or "Uncle Al."

The year before Al joined Penske, the team had been all-powerful with a new car called the PC10. Rule changes designed to reduce the amount of aerodynamic downforce generated by the cars worked against the successor to the PC10, and with Penske's PC11 neither Al nor teammate Rick Mears could match the new March cars. In the middle of the year, Penske produced a new batch of cars, called the PC10B, and in spite of the team's problems, Al was able to win his first Championship since 1970. He took the point lead with his second-place finish at Indianapolis after a late-race battle with Tom Sneva and was also runner-up at Atlanta, Milwaukee and in the Michigan 500. In mid-summer, amid intense heat and humidity, he won the inaugural Cleveland airport road race, ending a 37-race winless streak.

After finishing fourth in the season-closer at Phoenix, Al receives congratulations from Gordon Kirby on winning the 1983 national Championship.

Photo by Marc Sproule

Left

"This was in 1984—Karen and me—when I was with Penske running the Miller car."

AL UNSER

Photo Courtesy of the Unser Family

Right

"This is Mini Al (on a hunting trophy of Al's located in the foyer of his Albuquerque home)."

AL UNSER

Photo Courtesy of the Unser Family

In the second half of the year with the PC10Bs, Al and Mears had an even tougher time against the fast-developing Marches and Mario Andretti's Lola. They even were faced with John Paul, Jr.'s team VDS Penske PC10 winning that year's Michigan 500 after a spectacular battle with Mears. Ultimately, Al took the title by five points from a closing Teo Fabi with a string of fourths and fifths. At the final race in Phoenix, Al qualified eighth and fought his way into fourth place at the finish, two miles behind race-winner and Championship rival Fabi. "Man, that thing was as loose as a goose!" declared the sweat-laden, elated Al as he strode down the pit lane towards the post-race victory celebrations. "But we did it!"

Later he reflected on his hard-won title. "I'm still not happy, winning the Championship and not being more competitive in the last races of the year. Even though I won the Championship, it's not a fulfillment within myself because I was disappointed with both myself and the car right there at the end. But you know, all of us—Penske, Bob Sprow (Al's chief mechanic that year)—all of us would say as we started each and every race—and this was from the first race of the year—remember the points. We wanted to win the Championship. And with Penske, you can do that. You can take that approach."

The following year, 1984, was even tougher for the Penske team as new cars from March and Lola totally eclipsed Penske's new PC12. After the opening two races of the year, the PC12s were retired and replaced for Indianapolis by a fleet of new Marches. In fact, Mears won the 500 in his brand new March with Al finishing third. Things appeared to be looking up, but it wasn't to be. Mears came close a couple of times but didn't win another race before crashing at Sanair, Quebec, in September and breaking both feet. Al was never happy with that year's March, though he was competitive in some races, a mid-field runner in others. He finished third at Road America and fourth at the 200 mile sprint race at Michigan where he led for a few laps. At Caesar's Palace in Las Vegas, the site of the season's final race, Al battled for the lead with Tom Sneva only to crash out of the race in a controversial incident involving Sneva. In a perverse way, it was a fitting end to an unhappy year of racing for Al, which saw him finish no higher than ninth in the points.

"This is Buddy Baker's car at Watkins Glen in 1986. And the transmission was going bad and the brakes were no good, and I went down in the first corner. I was trying to use the transmission to slow down, and I didn't make it, and I had to spin it. That's all. I went there to run the IROC car, and Buddy Baker asked me if I wanted to run his car because he didn't like the road courses. And it's a good race car so I said sure, that I'd do it. I jumped in and qualified good and all that. It just wasn't set up for the road courses."

AL UNSER

Photo Courtesy of the Unser Family

194

In 1986, Al introduced yet another engine to Indycar racing when he drove Penske Racing's Chevrolet-powered PC15.

Photo by Art Flores

Meanwhile, Penske's eye had been caught by Danny Sullivan, the winner of three races in 1984 while driving for Doug Shierson in his rookie season of Indycar racing. Penske decided to hire Sullivan to replace Al while offering Al the job of being a stand-in for Mears if the latter wasn't recovered from his foot injuries in time to start the season. In the end Al agreed to drive for Penske for sure in the three 500 mile races. The rest of the season was on a wait-and-see basis.

The only race before Indianapolis in 1985 was the street race at Long Beach. There Al drove in place of Mears whose feet were too tender to suffer the abuse of a road race. Al finished fifth at Long Beach and then qualified a respectable seventh at Indianapolis. In that race, he ran with the leaders all the way, finishing four seconds behind teammate and winner Sullivan, and two seconds behind runner-up Mario Andretti. On his first pit stop, Al had been given a one lap penalty for brushing an air hose and the penalty dropped him to fourth, officially listed a lap down. Mears ran at Indianapolis, leading briefly before a transmission failure stopped him. He also ran the next race at Milwaukee and Al was on hand but not with a race car. The next three races were all road races, however, so that Al was back in the saddle aboard Mears' car.

This one-two finish at Phoenix in 1985 by the Als, Senior and Junior, set up the father-son season-end struggle for the 1985 Championship. Senior and Junior were the only drivers in contention going into Miami and the season finale.

On the podium after Miami, new national Champion Al withstood a drenching as he doused Al Junior like he had doused his son's hopes for his first Indycar crown.

195

Roger Penske (right) in conference with Penske crew chief Derrick Walker (left) and Al.

He finished fourth at Portland, Oregon, and then at the Meadowlands in New Jersey and the Cleveland airport race, he recorded a pair of thirds. In both races, his son Al Junior was the winner so that for the first time father and son were together on the victory podium. Then, at the Michigan 500, Al had an excellent run, leading the race and finishing a close second to Emerson Fittipaldi. Following a late-race caution flag, the race finished with a two lap sprint to the flag during which Al attacked Fittipaldi only to be blocked by a lapped car driven by old sparring partner Tom Sneva.

Thereafter, Mears ran only the Pocono 500 (in which he won with Al third) and the sprint race at Michigan, leaving Al to run all the remaining races. At Laguna Seca in October, Al finished an excellent second to Bobby Rahal after a fierce race. Then at Phoenix the following week, with Mears sitting out the race and helping Al make set-up decisions, the old man came through to score an excellent win. He qualified on the pole, slipped to third at the start and then came storming back, stealing

"IROC is a good series. It's a hard deal. They try to make all 12 cars equal. They can't do it but they work very hard at it. These cars—you can ask any NASCAR guy, he'll say it's the biggest piece of junk because they're not total, total race cars. They're Camaros, and they can't take a basically stock car and make it a race car. And that's not the object. They try to make 12 cars equal. So, you know, they do a good job of what they try to do.

"It is fun for the drivers. When you get a good car, and everything goes right for you. It's very enjoyable. It's fun because you can run very hard and it's serious. You know, you're talking about big dollars so it becomes very serious."

AL UNSER

Photo Courtesy of the Unser Family

the lead from Rahal and running away to a strong victory. In doing so, Al lapped the entire field, including Al Junior who finished second. That result meant that Al and Al Junior went to the year's final race at Tamiami Park in south-western Miami as the only drivers in contention for the Championship.

"I think that has to be the biggest thrill I've ever had," says Al. "Being in the winner's circle with Al (Junior) at the Meadowlands and then Cleveland and then the race at Phoenix and doing what we did in the Championship. That's got to be something that always will be the highlight of my life."

■ *"I don't think about (retirement). I know there will be a day when I'm going to have to quit. I'm not anything special and there will come a time when I won't be competitive or have the desire and when that time comes, I'll have to quit.*

"I've always said if you don't have the desire and the drive to go after it, then why do it? You're going to end up just making a fool of yourself. I definitely would hate to be called a has-been which I probably already have been called. But I mean me feeling that directly. I think every man is his own worst enemy on figuring out when he should quit. You can always have excuses why you're not going fast enough or why this or that isn't happening. So even for me to say I'll quit when I become uncompetitive or don't have the drive, I might have an excuse that tells me why. So I don't know what to say about quitting. One day it'll come."

197

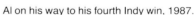

Al on his way to his fourth Indy win, 1987.

Photo by Bob Tronolone

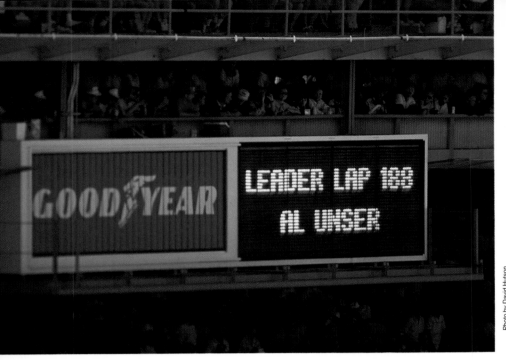

Photo by David Hutson

From no ride to *the* ride.

Al Junior embraces his father as Al begins his victory lap at Indianapolis.

Photo by Bill Stahl

In order to win the Championship, Al Junior had to finish two places ahead of his father in the final race of 1985. They qualified in eighth and twelfth places, son ahead of father. At the start they survived a first corner tangle which took out three frontrunners, and settled into the 200 mile road race in sixth and eighth places. For a while Al kept his son in sight but Junior slowly began pulling away, picking up more time and a place with a very quick pit stop. Senior made up one place on the race track and hung on, surviving a momentary, heart-stopping engine stall while leaving the pits after the first of his two planned pit stops.

Late in the race, the two Unsers had moved up to third and fifth places. As Sullivan drove away from Rahal to win the race, everyone's attention was focused on Al Junior and Al who had top young Brazilian driver Roberto Moreno between them. Al Junior was too far behind Rahal to have any hopes of making another position but Al had Moreno in sight and a chance of one place and two more points—enough to beat his son to the title by a single point.

Finally with barely 15 miles to run, Al caught Moreno. Another four miles and Al made a perfect pass, outmaneuvering and outbraking Moreno. "A few laps before that I thought it would be hard to catch Moreno, let alone pass him," said Al after the race. "But when I got up to him I could see he was in trouble. I think he must've blistered his tires. When I passed him, I was able to put him in a position where he couldn't come back at me. After that, it was a case of hoping I wouldn't run into any trouble with traffic and could stay ahead of him."

And so it was. Al finished fourth, directly behind his son, winning his second Championship in three years.

"If I had pressed it any sooner," explained Al, "and Al (Junior) had anything left, then I would have been history because I had nothing more left in me. There was no way I could gather up anything more. So I tried not to do it until the very last. I took a gamble. If there had been a yellow flag, I was history. If there was more traffic, I could've been history.

Nineteen eighty-seven saw Al tackle the off-road course at Riverside International Raceway.

Photo by Erik Koster

From nightmare to dream come true.

Photo by Bill Stahl

"Al (Junior) will tell you that his stomach tightened up at the end of the race. Well, mine tightened up when I got ahead of Moreno. I had made the point I needed. There was nobody between us. As soon as I got around Moreno, I saw Al up ahead. I never even looked at the scoreboard. I had no idea where I finished but it didn't matter because I had done what I needed to do, which was to finish just behind Al.

"I've got mixed emotions about this," he said in the immediate aftermath. "When I got the checkered flag and pulled up beside Al at Turn Two, I had a feeling that is hard to describe. It was a very empty feeling because I knew I had taken something away from him that I shouldn't have taken away. At that moment, I really would've preferred that he had the Championship.

"But during the race I was there to beat him. I had everything and everybody else behind me of course—the crew, the whole team. But I had to do it for myself. I had

Photo by John E. Biever

to do it. He was not going to give it to me, otherwise neither of us would be in the positions we are in. It's the same way I treated my brother Bobby when we were racing together. But I tell you, that feeling was a whole lot easier to handle than this one!"

So ended a remarkable year for Al. From part-time driver to Champion once again. And to have done it by racing against and beating his son. A very mixed bag of experiences and emotions.

Another facet of the story is that back in January of that year, Doug Shierson called and offered Senior a job with his team. Shierson had originally signed John Paul, Jr. for 1985, but the luckless Paul youngster was arrested for his involvement in his father's criminal activities. Thus, Shierson needed a driver. At the same time Al, Junior learned the new Winkelman/Lotus team he had signed to drive for was not going to happen.

"It's the Formula 5000 car either warming up or getting ready to take off for the race 'cause it has new tires on it. It had to be before practice started or the race. I thought this was a good series. I never understood why they discontinued it. The people were liking it, it was just starting to really get a hold. And then they put it to the Can-Am cars again, see, which, today, has lost its total prestige."

At Riverside in 1976, Al won the final F5000 race in convincing fashion.

AL UNSER

Photo Courtesy of the Unser Family

"Let's just say," comments Senior about Shierson's call, "that he called me and asked me who was around that he could hire. Earlier that same day Al (Junior) had called me and told me he had been released from his Lotus deal, and in the midst of our conversation, I told Doug that maybe he could hire Al. At the time, Doug had no idea that Al was without a ride. Doug had been asking who was available or if I was available. I told him I had already committed myself to Roger Penske. Doug asked me if I had signed a contract and I said, 'No, I gave my word of honor.' "

So it was that Shierson hired Al Junior and Al went into the season expecting to do only the three 500s and maybe one or two other races in place of the recovering Mears. Al says anyone who thinks he was unhappy with the deal he struck with Penske is wrong. "I made a deal and the deal I made was for three races. When I went into it, I knew what I'd done and I was not sorry in any way. I thought about it for quite a while and totally understood what I did. It's true that it was something that came up as a last resort, but I had other offers and I didn't want 'em."

"This is this year (1987) at Albuquerque with Mayor Ken Schultz (center), Bobby and myself and all the fans that showed up on Al Unser day. It was a very emotional day for me because it showed that you have a lot of friends and a lot of people in Albuquerque and the state of New Mexico that supported the Unser clan in racing. It just really made us all feel good for that many to show up. The parade was something else. It was neat, it really was."
AL UNSER
Photos Courtesy of the Unser Family

The same situation applied over the winter of 1985/86. There was some talk from other teams and individuals but none of them met Al's or Penske's standards. Once again Al decided to stay on as a backup, third-string driver behind Mears and Sullivan. In retrospect, the 1986 season was entirely anticlimactic for Al. He ran only five Indycar races, giving Penske's new PC15 and Chevrolet's new Indycar V8 their first runs in a race at the season-opener and continuing to race/test the new car/engine combination at Indianapolis.

He qualified in the middle of the second row but struggled with poor handling in the race, eventually falling by the wayside with a mechanical failure. At the Michigan 500 Al was aboard a Chevy-powered March and qualified second to teammate Mears. Engine problems slowed and then stopped him, however. More of the same with the March/Chevrolet meant he qualified poorly for the Pocono 500 and was then eliminated early in the race amid another driver's accident.

Once again it was winter and there was talk and rumor about who Al would drive for in 1987. Again, Al was interested only in driving for one of the top teams which narrowed his choices to four or five cars and those seats were already taken. In mid-winter Penske announced that he was going to run Danny Ongais in his third car at Indianapolis, and for the first time in 20 years, Al faced the start of a new racing season without a ride.

The accumulation of a Champion. Al Unser's home.

203

Photos by Tom Tennies

Come the first of May, he and Karen were on their way from Albuquerque to Indianapolis aboard their Newell motorcoach. Al checked into his condominium on the west side of town, drove the Newell over to the Speedway and parked it in "motorhome row" just outside the gates to Gasoline Alley. He began roaming the garages and pit lane looking, waiting, hoping for "something to happen. I had never been here before without a ride," he commented at the end of the month that included winning his fourth race at Indianapolis. "And I can tell you that was a very lonely, empty feeling."

Because he was interested only in an absolutely first-class effort, Al turned down an offer during the first week of practice to drive a Buick-powered car ultimately driven in the race by Gordon Johncock. There was even some talk of him driving a second car for '86 race-winner TrueSports, beside Bobby Rahal. But Al continued on foot until early in the second week of practice when he suddenly appeared once more, driving for Penske Racing!

In the first week at the Speedway, Danny Ongais had crashed and "rung his bell" badly enough that after a few days, the track's medical staff recommended that Ongais sit out the rest of the month. By this time, Penske had decided to retire his latest cars—known as the PC16—and regroup for the race with the March cars he had run in 1986. Mears qualified on the front row on the first weekend of qualifying driving a Chevy-powered March he had raced the previous year. Sullivan and Al qualified in the middle of the field on the second weekend. Sullivan's car had a Chevy engine, but there was no time to convert Al's car to take the new engine so he went to the starting line with one of the tried-and-true Cosworth engines.

The start of the Indy 500 is always a tense moment and so it was for Al in 1987. In the first turn, only seconds after the start, he was confronted by a spinning Josele Garza. "I elected not to get in there too hot," Al said later. Miraculously, there was no contact between Garza and Al, although the Mexican driver wound up in the wall, bringing out the yellow flag. On the restart, Al actually lost a couple of places, and on lap 17 he was lapped by polesitter Mario Andretti who was leading the race by a considerable margin. Then, on his first pit stop, Al uncharacteristically stalled his engine, losing more time.

"I had most of my trouble early in the race, in the turbulence behind all the other cars. I wasn't aggressive enough and I lost a lap to Mario, which was the one thing I did not want to happen. I was mad at myself for losing the laps, and when I killed the engine on the first stop, I had to say to myself, 'Come on Al, pay attention to what you're supposed to be doing!'"

Despite losing the lap to Andretti, Al was into the top ten by lap 50 (125 miles). Almost unnoticed, Al inched toward the front. By lap 60, he was into the top five and looking good for a strong finish. "From the second fuel stop I ran the car pretty hard," said Al. "We were a little short of steam down the straightaway but the handling was good. Once I adjusted myself to driving the car in the right way, we were strong.

"Let's not fool ourselves. There was no way I could run with Mario or (Roberto) Guerrero, but I was able to run with the fastest of the rest of them and the team had good pit stops—typical Penske— a good strategy."

As the final 100 miles came up, Al was a solid third behind Andretti and Guerrero. Then, barely 60 miles from the finish, Andretti's engine quit running. Guerrero took over the lead. Al, who had already made his last fuel stop of the race, was now in second. With 45 miles to go, Guerrero ducked into the pits for his last load of fuel. As he tried to leave the pits, he stalled. After restarting his engine, Guerrero was able to rejoin the race but at an agonizingly slow pace as he fought an overheated, slipping clutch.

Meanwhile, Al was taking the lead and motoring home through a final caution flag period and a four lap sprint to the checkered flag. By four-and-a-half seconds, he was the winner of this fourth Indy 500, equalling AJ Foyt's great record and also making him, five days short of his 48th birthday, the oldest man ever to win America's most famous automobile race.

"That last yellow really worried me," said Al. "Before that I was just trying to keep my distance to Guerrero. I had been having trouble in traffic, the car was pushing so bad. In the car after the checkered flag, I didn't believe it was really happening. My voice was trembling so much that I couldn't talk to Roger (Penske) over the radio or anyone else, for that matter."

Al ran two more races for Penske in 1987, the Michigan and Pocono 500s. Aboard a Chevy-powered March, he qualified sixth at Michigan and finished a strong second, and was running fifth at Pocono when his engine gave out. In September at the debut-race on the new one-mile track in Nazareth, Pennsylvania, Al drove for Vince Granatelli's team in place of injured an Guerrero. After qualifying tenth, Al charged up to second place only to be driven into the wall while lapping a slower car. Later that month at Laguna Seca, Al debuted Porsche's experimental Indycar and did some testing for the German auto manufacturer's new Indycar team.

Al gives no indication of a diminished desire to race and to win. While it could be said that, "He's done it all," Al seems intent on discovering what achievements his future must hold. At the time of writing, Al was expected to drive again on a part-time basis for Penske in 1988. It would be his 24th year of competing at the top level of American automobile racing.

"Daddy was the toughest mule you could ever find. He would never give up and he expected his sons to be the same way. He was a tough man to work for, but he taught you how to get the job done. You may think Bobby is stubborn and you can see it in Louie, too—he just won't give up. Whatever it takes. However many hours. And all that comes from Daddy. There's no doubt about it."

In the Victory Circle.

Photo by James Cutler

"I've always liked IROC. It's really an honor to be asked to go race IROC. That's one of those deals that ... I don know ... I watched Dad do it and then it was an honor for me to do it. IROC is neat.

Al Junior (#30) led his father (#5) across the Tamiami finish line—right into the 1985 Indycar national Championship.

Photo by Bill Stahl

The Fourth Generation: Al Unser, Jr.

"Nineteen-eighty-six was my first year and I was really happy just to be invited. And then to win Mid-Ohio—that was the first one I won—that was really, really neat. And then to win the Championship at New York ... I'm driving in my motorhome all by myself—Shelly wasn't there because she was pregnant— and I just couldn't believe it."

AL UNSER, JR.

Photos by Bill Stahl

Al Junior was standing in the kitchen of the old house he had bought a few months earlier. After racing Indycars for three years and finishing a very close second to his father in the 1985 national Championship, Al Junior had joined his father and uncle as a landowner in Chama, the small northern New Mexico town where the Unser clan has established its get-away homes.

"You see those mountains?" he pointed over his shoulder through the kitchen window, "That's what I want. A piece of mountain I can call my own. Most of the people up here who own a piece of land like that inherited it. But I'm going to get a piece of that mountain. That's what is so important to me about Dan Fogelberg's song, 'The Leader of the Band.' Dad taught me how to earn a living, how to earn enough money and freedom to buy something like that. And his dad taught him."

Thus far at least, Al Junior is the truest third generation incarnation of the Unser family. Like his father and uncles he was raised as a race car driver, exposed at a very early age to machinery, mechanics and racing. With the help of his family, he quickly established himself as one of the top drivers of the time: a recent winner in

Indycars, IMSA GTP cars and IROC stock cars. Al Junior is recognized as a clean, smart driver and—like father and uncle—a tenacious competitor.

Although he has yet to win the Indianapolis 500 or a national Championship, the ability to do so is undoubtedly there. Al Junior was runner-up to his father, of course, in the 1985 Indycar Championship and has won four races over the five years he's raced Indycars. He's finished second or third in 17 other Indycar races through the '87 racing season. He's finished second, fourth and third respectively in the Indycar Championships of 1985, '86, and '87. During the course of his rapid rise to the top of the sport he won Championships in both Formula Super Vee and Can-Am sports cars and was part of the winning team of drivers in both the 1986 and '87 Daytona 24-hour race. Also, Al Junior won the 1986 IROC Championship and was runner-up in the '87 IROC series. A particularly satisfying win in 1987—a year in which he was winless in Indycars—came in the IROC race at Michigan International Speedway, where Al Junior beat NASCAR star Darrell Waltrip to the line with a perfectly timed, last-corner passing maneuver.

"That was a pretty special race for me," says Junior. "It was the first major Championship race I've won on an oval. I came up through Sprint cars and won a lot of Sprint car races on ovals. My first year in a rear-engined car was in a Super Vee in 1981 and I won two oval races that year. But that was the last time I won on an oval until the IROC race at MIS.

"I love racing so much that I wouldn't be happy doing anything else. I've been around the racing environment so long that I know I couldn't do anything else and be happy. If I was to be put into a wheelchair tomorrow, I would work on being a designer of a race car because I would still want to be involved in racing and try to live racing the way I have as a driver."

209

This is at Milwaukee in 1983—a kid holding a kid, absolutely! I was so happy Indy was over. I got booed at this race because of what I did to Sneva."

AL UNSER, JR.

And Kevin Cogan came up and said, 'Thank you, Al. Thank you, Al,' because before he had been booed."

SHELLEY UNSER

As far as thinking about what happened at Indy that year, I still feel I was right. I'd do it again."

AL UNSER, JR.

Photo Courtesy of the Unser Family

"It's the old house, Christmas. I still have baby fat on me!"
AL UNSER, JR.
Photo Courtesy of the Unser Family

"I don't know what grade this was but this is a school picture."
AL UNSER, JR.
Photo Courtesy of the Unser Family

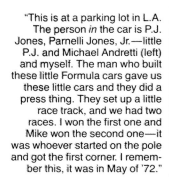

"This is at a parking lot in L.A. The person *in* the car is P.J. Jones, Parnelli Jones, Jr.—little P.J. and Michael Andretti (left) and myself. The man who built these little Formula cars gave us these little cars and they did a press thing. They set up a little race track, and we had two races. I won the first one and Mike won the second one—it was whoever started on the pole and got the first corner. I remember this, it was in May of '72."
AL UNSER, JR.

Photo by Earl Garretson

211

"My first mini-bike! My first brand new mini-bike! And I was grounded, believe-it-or-not! He (Al) got it out and showed it to me. The night before I got in trouble and he gave me a choice: I could have a spankin' or be grounded for a week, or something like that. So—I generally got out of all my groundings about half way through because of Mom—so I picked the grounding and then I got back from school the very next day and Dad whips this mini-bike on me and says, 'But you can't ride it, you're grounded.' See, he won't let me on it. See? That's why he's on it! This was 1969 so I was seven."

AL UNSER, JR.

"I was very fortunate to have a good car that day. Darrell Waltrip had to pinch his car down low in Turns Three and Four on the last lap, and I was able to capitalize on it. That was all there was to it. I had a good, strong engine in my Camaro and I just used my head so that everything worked out. It was neat—beating the guys in an IROC race always makes you feel good."

Al Junior is unlike most of the latest generation of Indycar drivers in having raced Sprint cars on dirt ovals. He did so when he was 15, 16, and 17, running all over the Southwest in World of Outlaws and other races. Despite his tender age, he was able to run with, and occasionally beat, the established stars of Sprint car racing. Particular success was achieved in a car owned and run by Walter Judge.

Before racing Sprint cars, going back to before his tenth birthday, Al Junior raced karts built and run by his father. Like Michael Andretti and many top European and South American Formula One and Indycar drivers, Junior's formative years aboard his dad's karts made him a racing veteran by the time he was a teenager. In company with his subsequent Sprint car experience, Al Junior was prepared in a thorough and unique

"This is an AP photo in '74, about my third year of racing. That's Larry Bond (Al's mechanic), back there, wearing a cowboy hat, and my dad. We're just starting racing. That's a Stinger by Bug, you set off to the side. This is when we first started getting into it.

"Doing this really did help me develop. I knew what a push was by the time I was 10, and what 'loose' meant, and what an apex was. I was nine when I started.

"That's a Viceroy helmet. I have tape on the helmet there to hold the helmet together because I went out on my mini-bike and crashed and the mini-bike came down on the helmet, broke the helmet and everything. Thank God I had a full-face helmet on or it would have really messed me up."

AL UNSER, JR.

Photo Courtesy of the Unser Family

way for a transition, at 18 years of age, to paved racetracks and rear-engined cars. Two years later he was racing Indycars, leading six races in his rookie year and scoring his first Indycar win the following year.

"When I started racing it was because my dad wanted me to race," he makes the point. "I did it for my dad. I've always wanted to win and I think that's what it all comes down to. I've always raced and wanted to win. I've never done anything else, nor have I wanted to do anything else. But like I say, I raced for my dad. It wasn't until, I think, my second year at Indianapolis that I wanted to do it for myself. It didn't happen until then. I had been racing for a long time by then, but I was still a kid. At Indianapolis in 1983, I was 21 years old. I was very immature in some ways, and I guess very mature in other ways. Those things seem to balance out overall, but, well, I raced for my dad for a long time because I wanted approval from him.

"I was never in conflict with my father or rebelled against him when I was growing up. And that correlates to our relationship now because at a racetrack we are more partners than anything else. To have had him on my side is really a great help, a great plus. It's why I am where I am today because of my father."

"This would have to be 1976 because I'm wearing a Viceroy shirt. That's at PIR—Phoenix. I was messing around in the pits. See my old bells—see?"
AL UNSER, JR.
Photo Courtesy of the Unser Family

"I'm 16. And I'm just sitting in it. The guy wanted to take a picture of the two of us (Al and Al Junior). I never drove the car."
AL UNSER, JR.
Photo Courtesy of the Unser Family

213

"This is during practice at Erie. That's Bobby Junior (#92) and me (#61). God, look how small I am there! Scary! Scary! The car I'm driving is a Maxwell chassis and has a bolt-on roll cage. It's an old car."

AL UNSER, JR.

"This was my first race at Erie, Colorado. And I crashed before I ever even raced … during hot laps. And then that was it. This was the first time Bobby Junior (left) and I raced against each other in the big cars, the Sprint cars. But then we didn't race because I crashed."

AL UNSER, JR.

214

After Al's father and mother were divorced, he lived with his mother. Wanda later married Bob Patcha and, these days, takes care of her son's books and helps manage his daily affairs. Back in his teenaged years, Al Junior had to consciously one day make the decision that he wanted to become a race car driver. To fulfill this desire, he determined that he had to move back to his dad's house.

"My mom spoiled me rotten when I was growing up," he admits. "I was the only son and the youngest in the family, so I had an easy road with my mom. When I was about 15 I realized that if I wanted to race, to try to be successful and to try to win Indy, I had to move in with my dad. And compared to my mom, he was a drill sergeant. But I had to do that in order to race. It was a small sacrifice, but at the time it seemed like a big sacrifice. My dad wouldn't let me go out and drink beer and chase girls. He kept me working on my go-kart."

Junior credits his six years of kart racing with teaching him about the basics of driving and racing. He says also that he discovered during those years how well he and his father communicate about the techniques of race car driving.

"The biggest thing I got out of karts," he says, "was that I started to learn about cars and how they feel and react when I was nine or ten years old. I also learned about racing, about how to use your momentum, how to let the guy you're racing have a little bit of room going into a corner so you can take a run at him coming off the corner.

"Working with Dad in the go-karts was really strange because we work so well together. He just has to say a few things to me, and I can go out and do exactly what he says. I'm able to think about what Dad is saying to me while I'm driving the race car and that started in go-karts."

From Al Junior's earliest days, of course, there was the presence across the street of his Uncle Bobby. As much as he was able to learn from his father, Al Junior was able also to learn from his uncle and to enjoy the enriching opportunity of being able to compare and contrast in an intimate way the approaches and styles of two of the most successful race car drivers in the history of the sport.

"This is Erie and it's a World of Outlaws show in 1978. No wonder a lot of people didn't think I was old enough to drive! That's (right to left) Lee Osborne, Rick Ferkel, Bobby Allen, Ted Johnson, Steve Kinser, and me. I'm the only one that looks ready to race! Hey, I'm ready to race, man. Let's go!"

AL UNSER, JR.

Photo Courtesy of the Unser Family

Junior describes his point of view on this unique situation: "When I was young, Uncle Bobby was quite a figure. He was my uncle, my dad's brother, and he drove Indycars like my dad. He was a strong figure in our family, and you knew that his shop was no place to be wasting any time. When I was a kid, I could never get anything about racing out of Uncle Bobby. I never even attempted to get anything out of him. If you went over to his shop, he would put you to work—sweeping, cleaning, doing something. And I didn't want to do that. Anytime I went over there and he'd ask me to do something, I would look up at him and say, 'I got to ask my dad first.' If he asked me to get the newspaper, I'd tell him I had to ask my dad."

In 1982, a few months before his first Indycar race, Al Junior drove his uncle's front-engined dirt car at Pike's Peak. It was his sec-

ond time at the Peak, and the first and only time that he has driven one of his uncle's cars. At 20 years of age, he finished fourth, a prelude to his record-setting victory the following year aboard a new, rear-engined machine. Bobby was there to oversee Al Junior's winning run in '83, but in 1982, it was Bobby's car that Junior drove, so it was Bobby who made all the decisions.

"That was quite an experience," says Al Junior. "I guess I was able to give him answers to questions right away that he hadn't been

able to get from my cousin, Bobby Junior. He naturally compared me to Bobby Junior because my cousin had driven that car for Uncle Bobby many times, and Bobby Junior would have to think about what the car was doing, about what he was feeling, while I was able to answer these things right away and to add some things Uncle Bobby didn't expect to hear. I'd tell him things about what the car was doing—suggestions to put into his head. And you could see his gears just *going*—thousands of rpm.

"It was neat. I really enjoyed it because I could tell Uncle Bobby things and he would say, 'Ah! I know what it's doing!' And he would make a change to the car, and it would be better and better. We did magic things with that car at Pike's Peak. Now that I've driven for Uncle Bobby and become more mature, I feel like I can get a ton of help from him. Once you learn to talk man-to-man with Uncle Bobby, there's a lot he can teach you."

Another member of the Unser family to have a strong influence on Al Junior when he was younger was his cousin Bobby Junior. Although separated in age by six years, the two cousins went racing together, first in karts and later in Sprint cars.

"I first thought of driving race cars for a living," says Al Junior, "when Bobby Junior started racing go-karts. He was like a brother to me. I have no brothers and Bobby Junior was always like a big brother to me. When he started racing go-karts it kind of woke me up to competitiveness. That was the only reason I wanted to go to the go-kart tracks—to smoke my cousin off in warm-ups because we raced in totally different classes.

Seventeen-year-old Al Junior participated competitively during a CART weekend for the first time at Phoenix in March, 1979. The sanctioning for this particular event remains unknown.

Photo by Bob Tronolone

217

"This was 1979, my first time at Ascot. I didn't do any good. I never did good at Ascot. They drove 'em too sideways there."

AL UNSER, JR.

"Ooh, the big block ... Stanton's big block at Ascot. This is when I drove for Gary Stanton in '81. Matter-of-fact, this brings back good memories because this was sponsored by Valvoline and it was the only car I've driven sponsored by Valvoline other than what's com-ing up. I didn't drive it for very long, just until May and then I quit. We weren't going very well, at all. It was a nice car, though. Me and Stanton just didn't mesh. We just didn't hit it, that's all. So the car was slow. Uncle Bobby said I was washed up after just a couple months."

AL UNSER, JR.

"He had moved away from home for the first time. We were living together. It was bad, though. When he drove away from his dad ... God, it was bad. We had $600."

SHELLEY UNSER

"We moved my furniture into a U-Haul truck and we hooked 'em ... "

AL UNSER, JR.

"We had $600 and we put $450 down on an apartment and went and brought groceries. Al was making $500 a month and I was making $600 a month and we *barely* made it."

SHELLEY UNSER

"Oooh, awsome! End-over-end. This is at Erie in 1979, at the Nationals ... the night I met Shelley's brother. It was the first time I went to the hospital because of a wreck. I was just knocked out. I didn't spend the night but I went there because I had a concussion. It was the first time I ever got knocked dingy. Look, both arms are up in the air ... I'm knocked out there."

AL UNSER, JR.

"When he first started racing, the enthusiasm that he had was just unbelievable. I mean, it was gung-ho racing. It was—'We're going to beat, these guys and never let up.' He'd talk about how much he loved racing and that's when I fell in love with the sport. I think I was about 14 at the time, and a year or two later I got into the Sprint car. Then I really had to make up my mind because I was in a real race car. I still had that enthusiasm that Bobby Junior gave me and I've had it ever since."

Now that he's an established Indycar driver, Al Junior looks back with nostalgia on his years of Sprint car racing. "I kinda wish I'd stayed in Sprint cars a little bit longer. I miss Sprint car racing because it was so much fun. I really enjoyed running on the dirt and I'd like to be able to do it all again because I think I could do a much better job now. I was very young when I was running Sprint cars, and I think I've learned a lot since then. At the time, I wanted to get out of Sprint cars. I wanted to get into asphalt tracks and do some road racing. But now I kind of miss the local Saturday night races. They were a lot of fun."

"This was the only race me and Stanton won. And it was the first one. That's at El Centro in 1980. It was a TV race, ESPN. We smoked 'em. Shuman started on the pole, and they said it was all Shuman, but we smoked 'em, flat out smoked 'em. That's the big block."
AL UNSER, JR.

"What I remember is the day before in practice was the first time I watched a Sprint car flip . . . right in front of me. And the guy got hurt bad."
SHELLEY UNSER

"Every time Bobby Junior went to El Centro he was on his head."
AL UNSER, JR.

Photo Courtesy of the Unser Family

At the 1981 Super Vee title recognition dinner, Al receives the Series Champion's trophy from Bosch's Ben Bendixen and says a few words to which Jo Hoppen (right) listens intently.

Photo Courtesy of the Robert Bosch Company

Leaving the Sprint car arena, in 1981 Al Junior, driving his Galles Chevrolet Super Vee, tackled the intricacies of formula racing on the road courses such as Road America ...

Al Junior started his first race in a rear-engined car aboard a Super Vee in September of 1980 and then ran the full Super Vee season in '81. Driving for Rick Galles, he won four of nine races and took the Championship. Then, staying with Galles, he moved into the SCCA's Can-Am series in 1982. In Galles' powerful Can-Am car, he was equally successful, once again winning four of nine Championship races. In the end, he beat experienced and much older road racers Al Holbert and Danny Sullivan to the Can-Am title by winning the final race of the season.

"Super Vee gave me rear-engined experience," explains Al Junior. "What I learned was to try to drive the car as straight as possible rather than hanging it out like a Sprint car. I also learned the

basics of road racing in Super Vee. When I got into the Can-Am, the biggest new thing for me was working with the heavy springs. Can-Am cars are closer to Indycars than a Super Vee in having very high spring rates. You don't have the ton of horse power and sustained high speeds of Indycar racing in a Can-Am-type car, but you do get used to the heavy springs, very stiff suspension and that kind of feel. It's completely different than the soft spring setup of a Sprint car."

Toward the end of 1982, before wrapping-up the year's Can-Am title, Al Junior started his first Indycar race. Driving a March owned by Chicagoan Jerry Forsythe, he finished an impressive fifth in a 500K race at Riverside, California. "That was great. I had a tremen-dous time," enthused the 20-year-old debutant after the race. "I was able to run with most of the guys, and I could outbrake almost anybody."

After winning the Can-Am Championship, Junior moved full-time into Indycars, continuing with Rick Galles who was determined to establish himself as a top Indycar team owner. Galles had taken Al Junior from Sprint cars to Indycars in the space of two years, providing the depth of support that few young drivers are able to enjoy at such a critical stage of their career. A successful Albuquerque automobile dealer and property developer, Galles is the son of H. L. Galles who established the family in the automobile sales business and long supported his son's deep involvement in racing.

■ *"The heaviest G loads I've ever felt were in a Sprint car, mainly because you sit so high and there's so much lean and roll to the car. You get on a short dirt track of a quarter-mile or less in length and the loading on you is heavy. I remember my first World of Outlaws race at a tiny little track in Lawton, Oklahoma. There was no straightaway. It was just a bull ring. It was 50 laps around that place and my head just fell off, the loading was so great. Physically, a Sprint car is harder to drive than something like a Super Vee or Can-Am car. An Indycar is different because the races are so much longer and that makes it a little more of a handful than a Sprint car. An Indycar is definitely more physically and mentally demanding than a Sprint car, but you can get worn out in a real hurry running a Sprint car on some of those bull rings."*

221

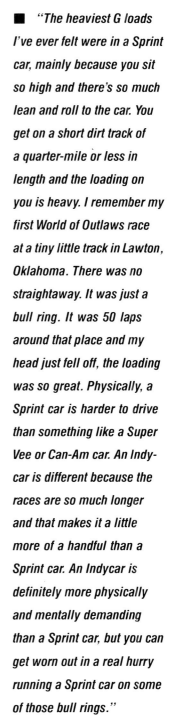

Photos by Marc Sproule

... and the ovals such as Milwaukee, winning the Super Vee Championship.

"Pike's Peak, 1982 with Bobby Junior. That was the year I drove for Uncle Bobby. I finished third. I got Rookie of the Year, 1982. That was my first year for competing. I went up there before and I didn't make it."

AL UNSER, JR.

Photo Courtesy of the Unser Family

"I love this picture ... I remember that shirt! Laguna Seca thinks they own little Al because his due date was the same as (the Indycar event at) Laguna Seca and I went because I wasn't gonna miss the race. The Laguna Seca course workers had a meeting before the race because they *knew* I was gonna have that baby there and they knew I wouldn't have time to get to any hospital. So they had it all planned. We celebrated his first birthday there, too, with the corner workers and the crew. "

SHELLEY UNSER

"We have to say that all the Laguna Seca corner workers are godparents of Little Al."

AL UNSER, JR.

Photo Courtesy of the Unser Family

Photo by W. H. Murenbeeld

In 1982, Al Junior, having conquered Super Vee, moved into the Can-Am, still under the aegis of Rick Galles.

222

"This is Road Atlanta, my first Can-Am race and the first one I won. Shelley's (behind Al) pregnant. And Rick (Galles, left) is going, 'Alright pard!'"

"I drove for Rick one year in Super Vee, one year in Can-Am and two years in Indycar and that's who I'll be driving for in '88."

AL UNSER, JR.

Photo Courtesy of Rick Galles

Al Junior, his mirrors filled with Danny Sullivan (#5), closes on Jim Trueman, founder of True-Sports, who signals his expectation of a pass by Al.

At Laguna Seca, Al shares a pre-race moment with Al Junior. Al Junior won the race and the Series Championship.

"This is 1982 at Riverside, my first Indycar ride. The Forsythe brothers owned it. Huey Absolom worked on it. I finished fifth. It was a neat race. This was with 52 inches (of boost), too—a lot of horsepower.

"I had to pass a rookie test for CART on a Wednesday. And then I went up and raced my Can-Am car at Laguna Seca that comin'-up weekend. And then the very next weekend was Riverside. And I passed the test and then we just showed up and raced.

"It was what I'd hoped and it wasn't. Everything about the Indycar was challenging because we were running up front in the Can-Am cars and (in the Indycar) I qualified 10th and so ... And I ran fifth and I raced with Dad—ran in *front* of Dad!

"That race made me realize that everybody was human up there. And it was a blow to know ... because right then I out-ran Tom Sneva who was somebody special to me, and Rutherford, and Gordon Johncock, and all these guys who I'd looked up to my whole life. I went out and out-ran them the very first day! And so it was no fun.

"But then, you know, that was on a road course, too. Put me on an oval and it would have been a different story. I knew that then—probably didn't realize it—but I knew that then. And when we got on an oval, they smoked me. My second race was Atlanta, and I almost missed the show."

AL UNSER, JR.

Not yet 21 years old when he drove the Forsythe brothers' March 82C and the winner of two highly competitive Championships in two years, Al Junior moved into Indycars in 1983.

Photo by Bob Tronolone

This is '83 at Pike's Peak. This is the year Bobby Junior and me were on the same team. We're going up to qualify. (Al Junior posted the fastest qualifying time.)

"The relationship between me and Bobby (Junior) is good, always has been. He's my older brother."

AL UNSER, JR.

Photo Courtesy of the Unser Family

"This is Pike's Peak in '83, on my way to a win. I haven't been back since but I'll go back up there again someday."

AL UNSER, JR.

Photo by Action Photography

"This is 1984." (No further explanation necessary.)
AL UNSER, JR.
Photo Courtesy of the Unser Family

For his move with Al Junior into Indycars in 1983, Galles struck a deal with Dan Gurney's All-American Racers to run one of that year's Eagles with a Cosworth engine rather than the Chevrolet power-plant preferred by Gurney's own team. After a slow start to the year because of the late arrival of the new Eagle, team and driver hit their stride in the middle of the summer. Al Junior led five races with the Eagle but was rarely a healthy finisher. In the middle of the year, Eagle designer Trevor Harris was fired, largely on Junior's instructions, and in two races the team ran a March instead of an Eagle. It was with the March, in fact, that Al Junior scored his best finish in his rookie year—a second in the Pocono 500. In hindsight, incidentally, Junior says his recommendation to Galles to fire designer Harris was, "the biggest mistake I've made in my racing career."

Bobby (left) and Al Junior confer with Rick Galles (center) while holding up the Phoenix pit wall.

On Portland's victory stand in 1984, Al Junior and Shelley celebrate Al's first Indycar victory.

Photo by Marc Sproule

Photo by Marc Sproule

Photo by Dennis Torres

"This is my first Indycar victory. At Portland on Father's Day in '84."

AL UNSER, JR.

"Look at his hands. Both hands up in the air. He almost crashed because he put both hands up!"

SHELLEY UNSER

"I didn't even know I was leading the race until he presented me with the white flag and then I came around and was wondering, 'Well, maybe . . . ' and I'll be damned! The radios were broken and we were going off the board.

"It was a real good feeling. It gave my stomach a real good feeling."

AL UNSER, JR.

"He and his dad were hugging and crying in the press room."

SHELLEY UNSER

Photo Courtesy of the Unser Family

Al Junior also ran at Pike's Peak in 1983, teamed with cousin Bobby Junior in a pair of rear-engined Sprint cars. (The two machines were owned by Denver architect Thad Woziwodzki and prepared by veteran mechanic Red Herman, who has worked with the Unsers at various times over the years.) Bobby Junior set a new record in practice, while Al Junior came through to win on raceday, also setting a new record. It was his third and, thus far, last appearance at Pike's Peak.

For the 1984 Indycar season, Galles decided to run March cars and he also fielded a second car in the 500-mile races for Tom Gloy. Junior was able to win his first Indycar race that year, on Father's Day in Portland, Oregon, and had a handful of other good finishes. In half the races, however, his car failed him, and in September he decided to leave Galles' team to take a tempting offer to drive the new Lotus Indycar. The Lotus was supposed to be bankrolled and fielded by Englishman Roy Winkelmann who had run a Formula Two race team in Europe many years before. But by January of 1985, the inscrutable Winkelmann had vanished, and Lotus released Al from his contract.

For twenty-four hours things looked bleak for Junior. There he was in the middle of the winter without a ride and all the good Indycar seats already taken. But a curious twist of fate occurred when John Paul, Jr. was arrested for his involvement in his father's illegal life. Young Paul had signed to drive for Doug Shierson's team in 1985. Suddenly Shierson needed a driver. He called Al Senior who had reached a verbal agreement with Roger Penske to run the 500 mile races in 1985, and Senior told Shierson that Junior had been released by Lotus. In that very innocent, paternal way, Al had set up one of the most memorable seasons of racing father and son have ever experienced.

"I was on my way to Daytona to test for the 24-hour race," says Al Junior, "and I called Dad and told him I was out of the Lotus deal and that I needed a ride. Dad said, 'Well, if I could have 25 percent of the deal if I were to get you a ride, would you do it?' And I said yes, I would do it. And Dad said, 'OK, I've got you a ride!'"

"This was our 1983 Christmas card. The car was a gift for 'Mini Al' from Coors."

AL UNSER, JR.

"We still have it boxed up and put away. He hasn't been able to destroy that one!"

SHELLEY UNSER

"Raceday, that's raceday at Laguna."

AL UNSER, JR.

Photo Courtesy of Al and Shelley Unser, Jr.

Happy Holidays

THE UNSER FAMILY

Al Junior and his Shierson Racing Domino's Pizza "Hot One" receive attention during an Indy 500 pit stop. Al qualified 11th but failed to finish the '85 event.

Al Junior dressed and ready to go to work.

■ "On a dirt track, there isn't a race car driver like Dad. He used to be magic in a Championship dirt car. There was nobody as smooth as Dad in one of those cars. In any type of car, Dad is a very smooth driver. If I could get to be as smooth as him, I would be happy because I would have accomplished what I'm after, which is to be as smooth as Dad in anything.

"Uncle Bobby was the kind of driver who could take a car that wasn't working very well and drive it a little out of control. He could do that and make the car go faster than it should. That's the kind of person Uncle Bobby is. He'll make the speed happen. He's like Mario (Andretti). He'll make it happen. And I'm like Dad. If it doesn't come, it doesn't come. The car's gotta be right."

229

Driving for Shierson, Junior went on to have a strong year, leading five races, winning two times (the Meadowlands and Cleveland GPs), and putting together a string of seconds and thirds. Into the final months of the year, Junior stayed in the hunt for the Championship as did his father in his back-up role for Penske Racing. Then in October, at the second from last race of the year, father and son finished first and second at Phoenix International Raceway, eliminating all other contenders from the Championship stakes.

"I ran in second place that day," remembers Al Junior, "and I felt like I won the race. It was the race of races."

On the way to his eleventh-hour battle with his father for the '85 Indycar Championship, Al Junior had to weather the effects of a broken leg in an accident at Road America in August. While leading in the rain, Junior lost control, slid off the road and hit a guardrail. He broke one of the primary bones in his right leg and appeared at the Pocono 500 ten days later with his leg in a brace. He had to be lifted in and out of his car by Shierson's crew chief Dennis Swan, yet he led 58 of the race's 200 laps and beat both his father and Bobby Rahal into second place.

Ten weeks later, father and son were fighting it out for the title at a new track in Tamiami Park in southwestern Miami. Neither was exceptionally fast in qualifying, with Junior starting the race from eighth place, four positions ahead of his father. In order to win the Championship, Junior had to beat his father by two places. Thus, the scene was set for an intriguing pursuit match, father chasing son.

230

Photo by Paul Webb

"This is Pocono in '85, the first race after my broken leg. Dennis (Swann) lifted me in the car. This is probably the first practice session because I'm *looking* at that car."

AL UNSER, JR.

"Poor guy had to lift him every time, in and out, in and out."

SHELLEY UNSER

"That was the first time I'd spent any sheet time—the first time I remember ever spending the night in the hospital. It was for a week, a long time and it was no fun"

AL UNSER, JR.

"We took the screws from his leg just this Christmas (1987) and made them into tie tacks."

SHELLEY UNSER

"In '84 when I crashed at Michigan in the black car when Chip Ganassi took me off—that was the first time I ever lost control of the car running 200 (MPH). And that scared me. It was a scary, scary feeling, scared me bad. So, I finally crashed at 200, lost control at 200 and I got over it."

AL UNSER, JR.

"He said that when he first got into the car after he crashed he said that he'd sit there for a second and go, 'This is stupid! What am I doing here?'"

SHELLEY UNSER

Photo Courtesy of the Unser Family

At the first turn, a three-car accident involving Mario Andretti, Emerson Fittipaldi and Roberto Guerrero eliminated two of the cars that had qualified between Al Junior and Senior. Junior: "I knew I was in trouble when I came by at the end of the first lap and there parked against the wall were Emerson, Roberto and Mario—all of them out of it. I needed those guys to finish between me and Dad and already, they were all out of the race."

Getting down to the job, Junior steadily consolidated his position, helped by rapid pitwork from Shierson's team. In the closing stages of the 200-mile road race, Junior was running in third place, five or six seconds ahead of his father. Between them was Brazilian driver Roberto Moreno which meant that Junior was one point ahead of his father.

Junior recalls the day: "With about fifteen laps to go Dad was still behind Moreno and there I was in my own hole. I couldn't gain a spot. Danny (Sullivan) and Bobby (Rahal) were outrunning me, and there was no way I could catch them. I had been relying on Moreno who was out of sight from my mirrors so that I couldn't see anything going on behind me. All I could see was that I had four or five seconds on Moreno and that Dad was still behind him.

"I had been having really funny feelings inside my stomach from all the stuff about the Championship. That race upset me more than any other race. I guess the pressure and questions about who was going to win the Championship really got to me. In the last laps of that race my stomach was so tight, all I could do was just try to stay within the walls. That

Photo by Paul Webb

Al and Al Junior found themselves together in Phoenix' Victory Circle following the October, '85 Indycar event there. Al finished first, Al Junior was the runner-up. This was a momentous occasion for not only were the Unsers the first-ever father-son Indycar 1-2, they had also eliminated everyone else from the '85 Indycar Championship race with only one event remaining to determine to whom the crown would pass.

Photo Courtesy of the Unser Family

Photo by Marc Sproule

Going into the '85 season-closer, Al Junior and Shelley made it quite clear who it was they did not want winning the Championship.

Photo by Dan Bianchi

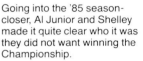

In the closing stages of the '85 season's final race, "Junior (#30) was running in third place, five or six seconds ahead of his father (#5). Between them was Brazilian driver Roberto Moreno (#6) which meant Junior was one point ahead of his father."

231

Photo by Bill Stahl

Al Junior (#30) led his father (#5) across the Tamiami finish line—right into the 1985 Indycar national Championship.

was all I was trying to do—just keep going. I had nothing more to give to the car or the race or the whole episode. I was in that hole and couldn't make any more points. So when Dad passed Moreno, I knew it was all over. I just ran the next four or five laps.

"Then my stomach relaxed for the first time in three days—since I had gotten off the airplane in Miami. I hadn't eaten, hadn't relaxed at all. The pressure got to me and I learned—I think I can say I learned more in that one day than in my whole career to that point."

After such a strong 1985 season, the following year was to be a disappointment for Al Junior and Shierson's team. Probably his best race of the year was at Long Beach in April where he qualified second and chased furiously after Michael Andretti to finish hard on his tail, still in second place. It wasn't until the very last race of the season that Al was able to win one, inheriting the victory after Roberto Guerrero's car ran out of fuel on the last lap. He was a distant fifth at Indianapolis. And he finished the Michigan 500 in eighth place, running on the apron, his car shorn of wings and with other bodywork damage after a late-race accident. Because he finished all but three races in 1986, Junior was able to eke out fourth place in the final point standings.

232

Photo by Art Flores

Photo by Erik Koster

Al Junior took time off from the rigors of Indycar racing in 1987 to do a little off-roading at Riverside.

233

Al Junior started off 1987 by teaming with Holbert Racing to win the 24 Hours of Daytona. The appearance of the winning team (left to right)—Al Holbert, Derek Bell, Chip Robinson, and Al Junior—seems to prove that you're never tired when you win.

The Al Unser, Jr. family awaits the 1987 visit of Santa Claus.

Photo Courtesy of the Unser Family

Al Junior's '87 Indycar look. He finished the season third in points, scoring six top-five finishes and was credited with a fourth place finish in the Indianapolis 500.

In 1987, Al managed to finish third in the points, but in reality the year was less successful because he failed to win a race. Nor did he lead until the final race of the year where he headed the field for a dozen laps at mid-distance and hung on to finish second (again behind Michael Andretti) in the best performance of the year for Al Junior and Team Shierson. Back in August, meanwhile, Junior had made the decision to leave Shierson's team and rejoin Rick Galles, signing a three year contract through 1990. Al felt Shierson's cars had not been quick enough on oval tracks in 1986 and '87 and was frustrated by qualifying poorly at many races. At the same time Galles was anxious to rehire Al, and it was Galles' enthusiastic personal and financial commitment which won the day.

"I made the switch to Galles Racing," explains Junior, "mainly because I think it is a very good team, a much better team than it was when I left three years ago. The desire Rick Galles puts toward winning is incredibly strong. He'll do anything to win, which is what a driver wants to see in a team owner. When I last drove for Rick in 1984, our team kind of fell apart. There was a second car involved and the team just didn't work well. Even in those days Rick was spending Roger Penske-type budgets, and there was no reason we shouldn't have won more races in 1983 and '84. Rick wanted to run a second car, however, and I think that really drained the team's resources.

"In the three years I drove for Doug Shierson, I continued to watch Rick and his team, and I think Galles Racing has progressed to the point where it's

Photo by Bob Tronolone

ready to become a front-running race team. Rick's team has not exactly dominated Indycar racing in recent years, but I think that getting back to the basics of running one car—which won Galles Racing and me the Super Vee and Can-Am Championships in 1981 and '82—will enable us to win the Indycar Championship. That's what Rick and I talked about in our negotiations and that's what we are going to do in 1988. It'll be a one-car team. Everything will be focused on that car.

"Rick also has a beautiful new shop, a wind tunnel, a shock absorber dynamometer, and many other good things. Best of all, the team is based in Albuquerque, so I can go to the shop whenever I like and work with the team on the development of the cars.

"It was very hard for me to make this decision because Doug Shierson's team is very good and successful. In fact, going into 1988, Team Shierson has won more races than Galles Racing. But I feel there is more potential for me with Rick's team. It took a lot of long, hard thinking to make this decision, but I want to go back home and race with the team with whom I've won two national Championships. We intend to regain the combination which enabled us to qualify so well and lead so many Indycar races in 1983 when I was a rookie. Rick knows what makes a winning team and I think that will happen again. I believe in the Chevrolet engine and I think this is the best move I could've made. I've signed a long-term deal with Galles Racing, and I think that will contribute toward giving the guys in the team the confidence that I'm here for the long run. We're going to make this thing work and win races and Championships."

Galles' relationship with the Unser family goes back many years. A former amateur road racer, Galles once sponsored Bobby Junior in Sprint cars and also helped Al Junior in his Sprint car days before setting up his own race team for the pair to successfully attack the Super Vee and Can-Am Championships. Al Junior and Galles have already achieved a considerable amount together, and the team owner and driver are close friends as well as neighbors.

These days Al Junior lives with his wife Shelley and two children in midtown Albuquerque. His house backs onto the Rio Grande and is about five miles from the family seat where his uncle and father reside. Al and Shelley, a native of Phoenix, met in 1980 when Al was racing Sprint cars. The pair was married in March, 1982, after a couple of years of courting.

Like his father, uncle and cousins, Al Junior is an avid snowmobiler and motor-cross bike rider. In the winter of 1987-88, on his property in Chama, he built a large workshop to rival his father's carefully maintained shop half a mile to the south. Working late at night in the off-season, Junior tunes and fiddles with his snowmobiles in constant competition with his father, uncle and cousins. As much as this is for fun and relaxation, you can see in Junior's enthusiastic, good-humored style of snowmobiling, the same type of resolve, persistence and even obstinacy that has made his family so successful. He should be a superstar for a decade or two to come.

"That's a go kart. I was 13 years old. That year we won about 36 straight asphalt races, I believe, and won both the Dirt and Asphalt Championships for New Mexico. It was really the last year that we ran solid in go karts.

Bobby and Bobby Junior with the red, white and blue Unser entry in the 1978 Pike's Peak Hillclimb.
Photo Courtesy of the Unser Family

The Fourth Generation, Continued

The latest Unser to join the auto racing fraternity full-time, Johnny Unser.

Photo by Dan Bianchi

"I started racing at seven and ran 'til I was nine and then quit 'til I was 12—Junior was running Sprint cars, and stuff—and then at 12 I started up again with go karts. We ran a year and then the second year back was when we won the Championship. It was a good year. Then we had one more year that we ran go karts on and off—not real steady—and then ran the stock cars, the full-size cars.

"Without go karts I wouldn't have known what to do in anything else. They didn't have a ton of horsepower and you didn't have a big car, but reflexes had to be just ungodly sharp and I learned a lot about car control."

ROBBY UNSER

Photo Courtesy of the Unser Family

Some other members of the third generation of racing Unsers have tried or are trying their hands at careers in racing. Bobby's oldest son, Bobby Junior, raced karts, Sprint cars and Super Vees and in the early eighties was a front-runner at Pike's Peak. He still races occasionally at the Peak but has otherwise retired from racing to work in the real estate business. Younger half-brother Robby has raced karts, stock cars, Sprint cars and Barber-Saab cars and made a successful debut at Pike's Peak in 1987. Cousin Johnny, the younger of Jerry Junior's two sons, has raced Russell-Mazda cars and quit teaching school in 1987 in order to go racing full-time

Bobby Junior is an effusive man who played drums in a rock 'n roll band during his school days. He was a popular and talented rock 'n roller, torn between his drums and race cars. He raced both karts and sprinters with his cousin Al Junior, who is six and a half years younger than Bobby Junior. At his best at Pike's Peak, Bobby Junior has focused on the mountain climb in recent years. In 1981 he set a qualifying record at the Peak and duelled with his cousin Al Junior in 1983 when the latter won the race. "I know the mountain as well as any man," says Bobby Junior, "and I can go fast up there. I've done well at the Peak and I feel good about the place. I enjoy myself when I go racing there."

Robby is a dozen years younger than Bobby Junior, a product of Bobby Senior's second marriage to Norma. Dark-haired and tall, almost gangling like his father, Robby has shown a lot of driving ability. In 1987, he bounced back from breaking a leg in a Championship dirt car to win the FIA's Group A World Hillclimb Championship. There were two rounds to the Championship, the first at Pike's Peak, the second at Oberjoch in West Germany. Robby won his class in both events. The course at Oberjoch is a real contrast with Pike's Peak, comprising 3.5 miles of paved road and 103 turns! "It's absolutely the twistiest road I've ever seen in my life," declares Robby.

Twenty years old in 1988, Robby stands as the next Unser in line to take a shot at a career in big-time automobile racing. Even though he knows he has large shoes to fill and a super-talented cousin to chase in Al Junior, Robby feels he is up to the task. Time will tell, of course. In the meantime, Robby offers these closing thoughts about his relationship with his father, uncle, half-brother, cousin, and life as a full-blooded, racing Unser.

"Daddy has always helped me with my racing," begins Robby. "It's because of him that I've enjoyed most of the opportunities I've had, and I'm sure there will be

239

240

"This is Bobby Junior. He was only about two years old, so this would have to be around 1957."
BOBBY UNSER
Photo Courtesy of the Unser Family

Just as his father and uncles before him, Bobby Junior competed at Speedway Park. Father Bobby works the jack during a stop for some impromptu body work.

Photo Courtesy of the Unser Family

242

Bobby Junior also tested his skills in Super Vee competition in 1978.

Photos by Bob Tronolone

"This is the kart I won all the races in. And that's Reggie Baldwin. He helped me go kart racing. At that time, Dad was still racing Indycars. And Reggie, he helped me. He's a good guy. He taught me a lot ... I don't know ... he taught me a lot about just being a person. I guess there's certain people you run across sometimes, that really help you. He wasn't really a great racer, you know. Dad's the one that made the race car go fast. But Reggie was just a really good friend."

ROBBY UNSER

Photo Courtesy of the Unser Family

"This is the trophy for the first go kart Championship I won. I was 12 or 13 right here."

ROBBY UNSER

Photo Courtesy of the Unser Family

more opportunities he'll try to open up for me. As far as driving the car is concerned, I find Little Al can help me out best if I'm having a problem driving the car. Sometimes I just don't understand Daddy's way of explaining. I think Little Al has an easier time of relating to me, of telling me what I need to know. Little Al is much closer to my age and he understands what I'm going through. Dad went through it but Little Al went through it more recently and is still, to a point, going through the learning stages.

"But now, if I need to know how to make the car go fast, then Daddy is the one who makes the cars go fast. He knows how to make the chassis right. I think I would tend to go strictly on driving problems to Little Al but on a handling problem to Dad, for sure to Dad. I mean, Little Al is smart but he doesn't even have the foggiest idea, compared to Dad, on the chassis. I mean, he knows it but not like Dad. In fact, I don't know anybody that knows it like Dad.

"I think Uncle Al has talent. Daddy, I don't know. I would say Dad is probably, according to him for sure, less naturally talented than Uncle Al. Uncle Al's so smart. Uncle Al, to me, reminds me of a wise man, like Moses, or somebody. He's so smart and he's calm and he knows when it's time and when it's not. He knows how to handle situations. He's great. In or out of racing. Life. Looking at Uncle Al, not knowing who he is, I would see the same thing, you know. It's not just that he's my uncle. Wise, smart human being.

"Dad's got a talent about mechanics that's unreal. Uncle Al doesn't. Dad can make machines and engines and stuff and it's amazing what he does with them.

"That's my first year in the stock car. I was 15 years old. We won nine out of 13 mains and won the NASCAR-sanctioned New Mexico points Championship. The four that we didn't win, three we didn't finish because of flat tires and the other one we finished in second place. We broke the track record by two-and-a-half seconds the first race (in Albuquerque at Seven Flags); we went to El Paso and won at El Paso; we went to Roswell and won at Roswell. Everywhere we went with the car, we won.

"There was a Winston Cup points Championship, and it had three main races. The first race of the season, which was a two-day event, the Governor's Cup and the Winston Fall Roundup. And we won all three of those. And I was the youngest one to win a New Mexico points Championship at the time. I think Daddy and Uncle Al were 16 and Little Al was 16 and I was 15."

ROBBY UNSER

Photo Courtesy of the Unser Family

245

"This is my first year in stock cars. Daddy was a lot of help to me. He owned the car, and we ran it out of the shop down here."

ROBBY UNSER

Photo Courtesy of the Unser Family

On November 25, 1983, Bobby and Marsha (far right) watch as Bobby Junior dances the first dance with his new wife, Tina.

Photo Courtesy of the Unser Family

246

"This is the stock car I drove in South Dakota—1983, '84. This is in Denver, Colorado. That was the year they had a stock car division that was open. I mean you could do anything: wings, all kinds of stuff. That car right there was faster than a lot of Sprint cars. In fact, at one time at a race track in South Dakota where I was hot-lapping, I out-ran a Sprint car. It was fast, a lot of horsepower."

ROBBY UNSER

Photo Courtesy of the Unser Family

"That's the same car in its second year. A different paint job is the only thing different. With that, we repeated everything we did the first year. We won the Championship—did a little bit more travelling. That same year, I drove another car in South Dakota while I drove this car. I flew up to South Dakota every Friday, flew back Saturday morning to race Saturday."

ROBBY UNSER

Photo Courtesy of the Unser Family

247

During the 1986 season, Robby explored the world of open-wheel formula racing, competing in the Barber Saab Pro Series. He finished fourth in the point standings, scoring a win at Brainerd International Raceway.

Photo by Tyler Photo Illustrators

248

"That's Jackson, Minnesota, right there, where the picture's taken. It was before a race. It's the first Sprint car ride I ever had. I guess this was 1984-'85. The man (leaning in the car) is Casey Luna, my car owner."
ROBBY UNSER
Photo Courtesy of the Unser Family

249

"This was my second race in Sprint cars. The first race was in Albuquerque, I ran second. That's Las Cruces and it was a clean sweep: the bash, the heat and the main. And the lady was a trophy queen. She was cute!"

ROBBY UNSER

Photo Courtesy of the Unser Family

Photo by Southwest Racing

Uncle Al is not that way and Little Al's the same. Little Al's good at the driving part but he's not as good at making his race car go fast, you know? He doesn't know the mechanics. I think I know the mechanics. I think I have more of a mechanical mind than a natural talent. I know God's blessed me with a certain amount of talents. They're different … say, like comparing me to Al Junior … Little Al's got certain things that I just don't know where he gets them. But I know I can have those same things. I'm just gonna have to work at it a little bit harder. But I have talents that Little Al doesn't have. And I can do things that he can't do.

"I think everybody in our family is talented. Really, it's pretty awesome when you sit down and look at the family. There's some really

"This is at Knoxville. We stayed in Knoxville and raced weekly for three months. Two weekends before this picture was taken, I had totaled the car. I took out some boards of the fence from the top down—a pretty bad wreck. As it turned out, this car (in the picture) was being built and what we were going to do is … The race where I wrecked was to be the last race on the car. It was sold. And I mean I totaled every, everything on the car except the block and the injectors. The headers, steering wheel, seat, seatbelts were ripped, all four tires were ruined, I mean everything! The wing, the front wing, the frame, everything! I couldn't believe it! It was pretty bad.

"But this, right here, this is my favorite picture because that car's hooked up. I'd say that was one of the best runs we had. The car is working right there, awesome. Really, really, really working."

ROBBY UNSER

Photo Courtesy of the Unser Family

Photo by J.R. Photos

talented human beings in the family. I mean everybody in our family, especially the men. We all do have something. I don't know what it is, but there's something that makes us all the same.

"I want to race, I want to be good at it—Indycars. Indianapolis and Formula One is what I want to do. Eventually, I'd like to have my own team and build my own cars. I want to be able to drive them as well as own them. I think eventually, some day, it would be nice for Al Junior and I both—Daddy and Uncle Al never ran on the same team. I want to see Little Al and I run on the same team.

"Daddy and Uncle Al, I think because they didn't run on the same team is why they're so good. Because most of what they did is against each other. I think that's what made the Unser family tick—

"This was our transporter, itty-bitty trailer. We didn't have very good motors. That was our downfall when I was running Sprint cars. Casey wanted to run a Ford, which he's doing now. And because he was saving up to do that, he wasn't putting money into good motors, which were Chevy motors when I was running. Now he's putting money in it but they're Fords. So, I don't know ... we'd have some bad runs like at Knoxville, at the Nationals—motor problems, a lot of motor problems—just no horsepower. And you just can't run with those guys without horsepower. And I mean you can see the trailer wasn't the biggest. We didn't have much to work with, actually."

ROBBY UNSER

Photo Courtesy of the Unser Family

"This is the day before I broke my leg (May 21, 1987). It's the first Midget I ever drove and it's at the Speedy Drome in Indy. Don Shepherd is on the left, Bill Roynan on the right. He owned the car and Don Shepherd used to own my dad's Sprint car. Dad's taking the picture.

"That was a Cosworth-powered car. The car was about a 10th place car from what I was told. Bill Roynan, who I've known for a while—really nice, nice guy, nice people—let me drive it that night. He likes to own it and work on it and he drives it sometimes. Anyway, we went from the second-to-the-last row, or something like that, and finished fifth, which ... It was a 100 lap main and I was dizzy for a while—literally. I mean, *literally*. I guess about eight to 10 laps before the end of the race, they had a yellow and I had to loosen my neck strap to shake my head because I was dizzy. It was a fifth-of-a-mile track, and I'd never been on anything that small. I'd never been in a Midget.

"The next night was the night that I had a ride in a Champ Dirt car at the Fairgrounds—from the smallest car on the smallest track to the biggest car on the biggest track. And I unfortunately got hurt (a badly broken leg) during that ride. That's the only time I've broken anything. It was the first time I drove a Champ Dirt car and we were doing really good—started dead last in the race because the starter wouldn't start on the car—the car was basically a junker but Daddy did some stuff to it and it was hooked up. I mean we were really hooked up. We had to finish 12th or 13th or better to make the main. So I'm running 13th, white flag, and crashed in Turn Three with another guy. The brakes didn't work on the car very good and the front end ... I'd passed half the field, I mean there was 30 cars started the race and it was only a 15 lap race, and I'd never been on (the track), it was the first time ever for me. So it was a good race. I mean, I was pleased with what I did but then unfortunately I got hurt."

ROBBY UNSER

Photo Courtesy of the Unser Family

Little Al and I've talked about it and we've pretty much come up with the fact that if it wasn't for the competition between the brothers—between Daddy and Uncle Al, Louie and Jerry—they wouldn't have been as hard-headed or tried to achieve as much as they have in their lives. The whole family has been in competition with other members of the family, not with other people we don't know. I mean, it's brothers and cousins, uncles, whatever. It's within the family.

"Now, our generation, Little Al, Bobby Junior and I, we have a different relationship than Dad and Uncle Al had. It's not quite as fierce competition. Basically, we're brothers is the way we look at it. I mean, we're gonna do whatever we can to help each other, which Daddy and Uncle Al do too. But, it's different, it's just different.

"Daddy thinks the reason I won't make a lot of mistakes is he chews me ragged. But now see, I disagree. I think I could make fewer mistakes if Dad was a little different. But that's what worked on him, see. And that's what his dad did to him. And see, Daddy, my Dad was Granpa's favorite, I believe. When Granpa died, Dad took over. I know that. Dad's way of life is Granpa's, his way of thinking about women, about kids, about the way life should be, about what you should do in life . . . Everything is his way.

"That was this past year (1987), my rookie year. Pike's Peak I drove with a broken leg. I had a cast on. I was on crutches. It was only a month-and-a-half after the rough break—a double compound fracture (from the Champ car accident). First of all, I wasn't going to drive because of my leg. But talking to Dr. Trammel—Dad did some talking—we figured out that they could make a cast that I could move my ankle forwards and backwards and my knee a little bit. And if there was a way for me to left-foot brake, I could work the throttle and run the race. So, I did. We ran it. I couldn't stop the car with my right foot if I had to, on the loose gravel road, couldn't lock the tires up. But there wasn't such stiff competition that I really had to get everything out of it. But I ran the car hard enough. I ran it hard—hard enough to win the race. But I didn't have to have my leg really 100 percent in order to do it. It was low horsepower, it was a momentum-type thing, and it was OK. It was a Mazda 323, a Rally car, basically an easy car to drive, not very fast. There wasn't a ton of competition in the race. But I won the race, nevertheless, or that division: Group A Rally Cars."

ROBBY UNSER

Photos by Art Flores

Photo by G. Paumann

253

"Pikes Peak was FIA-sanctioned and what-not. And there's another race in Oberjoch, Germany that, if you run both of them, between the two you get points for an FIA Hillclimbing Championship. And so Mazda didn't want to go over with me, didn't want to take me over to drive even though it could have meant they'd win the Manufacturers Championship. So Jo Hoppen of Audi took me over along with some other people from Pikes Peak, some other cars, and brought the car for me to drive and we won the race over there, too, and won the Hillclimbing World Championship. It was neat. Germany was probably the most fun I've ever had. I mean it was great. It wasn't a wild time. It was just really neat to see the country. It was clean, just ultra-clean and the people: You can't even believe how nice the people are."

ROBBY UNSER

Photo Courtesy of the Unser Family

Here's to the Unsers!
Being BEST is their way of life.

Mechanical Industries President Harold Hollnagel and Treasurer Judy Hollnagel are shown with a diesel engine exhaust manifold produced in the computerized numerical control machining center in the company's Milwaukee (Wisconsin) facilities. The Hollnagels and their 200 Mechanical Industries employees congratulate Bobby Unser, Al Unser, and Al Unser Jr. for their victories, their contributions to auto racing, and for being THE BEST in their business! Bobby Unser is automotive adviser for Mechanical Industries.

Being BEST also is our way of life at Mechanical Industries!

Being BEST is their way of life for the Unsers! They've driven more miles, racked up more victories, and earned more money in the famed Indianapolis 500-Mile Classic than any auto-racing family in history!

Being BEST also is our way of life at Mechanical Industries! For more than 40 years, we have been serving large and small manufacturers as THE BEST... THE TOP-QUALITY... outsource for components and custom fabrications and a broad range of metalworking and assembly operations.

We have grown successfully as a contract manufacturer because we consider it our responsibility to do the job the way our customers want it done... to exact specifications... on time... at a competitive price... to help our customers produce top-quality products for their customers.

In other words, to help our customers be THE BEST in their business, too!

MECHANICAL INDUSTRIES

8900 North 51st Street
Milwaukee, Wisconsin 53223
Telephone 414-354-8070

The BEST In Quality Contract Manufacturing

Robby receives his 1987 Intercontinental Hill Climb Challenge Cup trophy from (right) Jo Hoppen, Audi Special Vehicles Manager, and Robert Donner, Sr., the President of the Pike's Peak Auto Hill Climb Association.

Photo Courtesy of Audi of America, Inc.

"But Dad's done a good job with us, I think. I've learned things—not necessarily, I don't think, the way I would have liked to have all the time—but I learned them. And I learned some things his way I guess I wouldn't have learned otherwise. But Daddy ... it's kinda his way and that's it. That's the way it is. And OK, great! I can put up with it. That's what I chose for this life. I knew what was going to happen to me before it happened so I don't mind. I can live with it. I'm not saying Dad's right and I'm wrong or he's wrong and I'm right, I'm just saying I do have a different way I'm gonna approach kids and marriage. Daddy has taught me an awful lot about driving race cars and about life and I hope I can use everything he taught me in a way that's good for me and the people around me."

The Unser tradition carries on.

"That's Dad and me and a translator. Right there, what we're looking at, there's something like 50 Group A cars there, 14 or 15 different classes, and we're trying to figure out what class I'm in. See, in Europe, Group A, that's all there is and it's tough over there. In Germany, it's a different story. I had to run hard, real hard. I wasn't gonna win the race without it. We didn't beat all the Group A cars but we beat our class."

ROBBY UNSER

Photo Courtesy of the Unser Family

255

The littlest Al, Shelley and Al Junior's son, reaches for the checkered flag atop the Indianapolis 500 Borg-Warner trophy, perhaps a portent of the continuation of the Unser family tradition.

256